ADVENT OF THE

SEASONAL SERMONS AND PRISON WRITINGS
1941–1944

ALFRED DELP, S.J.

Priest and Martyr

ADVENT OF THE HEART

Seasonal Sermons and Prison Writings

1941–1944

English translation by Abtei St. Walburg
Eichstätt, Germany

IGNATIUS PRESS   SAN FRANCISCO

This book is comprised of selected texts taken from
Alfred Delp: Gesammelte Schriften, volumes 1, 3, and 4,
edited by Roman Bleistein, S.J., © Verlag Josef Knecht,
Freiburg im Breisgau, second edition, 1985,
and *Der Mensch im Advent* (foreword by Roman Bleistein, S.J.),
© Verlag Josef Knecht, Freiburg im Breisgau, first edition, 1984

Cover photograph: Jesuit Archive, Munich

Cover design by Riz Boncan Marsella

CONTENTS

The Christmas Vigil

FOREWORD

to the German edition of *Der Mensch im Advent*

Advent was one of the great themes that preoccupied Father Alfred Delp, S.J. (1907–1945), during his brief lifetime. The earliest text handed down to us from him is an Advent drama, *The Eternal Advent* (1933). The final Advent meditations, written on numerous small slips of paper and smuggled out of Tegel Prison in Berlin as he faced death, conclude the theme of Advent. That was Father Delp's Advent of 1944. Representing the years in between, we have a text from 1935 and sermons from 1941 through 1943.

The text from 1935 originated from a series of sermons directed against the "German Faith Movement", a neo-Teutonic, anti-Christian sect. Delp wrote this text while he was studying theology in Valkenburg, Holland. The sermons from 1941 through 1943 were preached at Saint Georg Church in Munich-Bogenhausen. Delp wrote the 1944 meditations in Tegel Prison, usually while his hands were in handcuffs. These meditations were smuggled out of the prison as secret messages. All of the texts presented here are taken from *Alfred Delp: Gesammelte Schriften*, volumes 1, 3, and 4.

Why did the theme of Advent so fascinate Alfred Delp? Presumably it was because in Advent an expectation becomes tangible, breaking through all encrustation, calling inflexibility into question, and above all, renewing the Christian and sending him on his way, on a new and unknown journey.

The mood of the Exodus, the certainty of the promise that applied to that departure, the joy of experiencing that God can be relied upon—all of these are essential to Advent. Delp's years had an Advent character primarily because they were filled with trouble and danger.

In this mood of expectation—confidence and doubt, insecurity and joy, audacity and certainty—the Delp of those days encounters the reader of today. Like those who lived through the war, there is one thing that we people living today know: man is a creature of Advent. He is under way.

At times, Delp's language may impede the encounter between author and reader. Nevertheless, anyone who enters into his testimony will be introduced to Advent as the time of great expectation and will set out upon the way again, filled with hope. The consolation of these texts is that they encourage us toward a new and blessed departure.

Roman Bleistein, S.J.
Munich, April 27, 1984

FOREWORD TO THE ENGLISH EDITION

I welcome this English translation of Advent texts by Father Alfred Delp, S.J. I would like to thank wholeheartedly those who made this publication possible and to congratulate those who will read it. As one of the last witnesses who knew Father Delp personally, I am very pleased that this book will make him better known in America.

A victim of the Nazi dictatorship has a difficult time being remembered when no "earthly" gravesite exists for people to visit as pilgrims. In Germany, there are now many schools, retirement homes, parish buildings, and other sites bearing Father Delp's name, but no real center for pilgrims, such as the tomb of Blessed Rupert Mayer in Munich.

What remain to us are the writings Father Delp left behind. From his imprisonment of more than six months, we have a treasury of writings that were smuggled out of the prison. Now, *Advent of the Heart* will begin to communicate Father Delp's spiritual and intellectual legacy to American readers. This book presents Advent sermons from Father Delp's parish work in Munich, alongside the powerful messages from his prison Advent experience of 1944. It is to be hoped that reading these texts will spark a desire to learn more about Father Delp.

The more one reads and reflects upon Father Delp's writings, the more one clearly recognizes the prophetic message for our times! Admittedly, to our fast-living era, Father Delp's language is not easy to read and understand. Nevertheless, like his Protestant contemporary, the theologian Dietrich Bonhoeffer, Delp ranks among the great "prophets" who comprehended the horror of Nazism and handed down a message to our times, insofar as our times are still able to comprehend and process prophetic words. It is worthwhile for us to reflect upon this message today.

Therefore, I wish this little book a successful journey, and I hope it will soon be followed by more of Father Delp's words of hope.

Karl Adolf Kreuser, S.J.
Munich

TRANSLATOR'S PREFACE

Perhaps the best introduction to an author is to read selected texts about a subject close to his heart. *Advent of the Heart* offers the reader just such an opportunity, presenting Father Alfred Delp's spiritual understanding of one of his favorite themes, Advent. This book was inspired by the 1984 German volume *Alfred Delp: Der Mensch im Advent (Man in Advent)*, edited by Roman Bleistein, S.J. (1928–2000), a collection of the Advent writings from the years 1935, 1941, and 1944.

Advent of the Heart combines the texts of *Der Mensch im Advent* with all other available Advent texts, as published in the most complete collection of Father Delp's writings, *Alfred Delp: Gesammelte Schriften*. For each week of Advent, two sermons preached in Munich are followed by an Advent message written in prison. For the convenience of the reader, each section begins with the pre-conciliar Latin liturgical readings and prayers in use at that time. The English translation of the liturgical texts presented here is based upon Father Delp's discussion of these texts in German, compared and corrected against German and English missal translations of the time. Where Father Delp quoted Scripture in Latin, the Latin is given first, followed by the English translation of his rendering of the text in German, if he did so. Where he offered no translation, an English translation consistent with his previous usage is added in brackets.

Additional material has also been added to aid the reader, including a biographical Introduction and a chronological summary of Father Delp's life, with selected historical events that affected him and those around him (Appendix 1). The only two Advent texts unrelated to the weeks of Advent are the 1933 Advent play *The Eternal Advent* and the sermon sketch "Advent 1935". These are placed after the Chronology as Appendices 2 and 3.

As the two forewords indicate, the original German sermon texts and prison writings are not a polished literary work. They were published posthumously, with only minimal corrections to preserve Father Delp's words faithfully. Their roughness evokes a powerful sense of immediacy rooted in the suffering and danger of the times. When read aloud, the rhythm and style of Delp's preaching become evident. It was a challenge to leave these qualities intact and still offer a clear and readable translation. New material and research published by Father Bleistein in the 1980s enables the German source texts to be understood and translated more faithfully to their original meaning than ever before. Great care has been taken to translate key words consistently and to identify literary, scriptural, or political references wherever possible. Father Bleistein's footnotes from *Alfred Delp Gesammelte Schriften* are translated in full, and additional notes by the translator are marked "TRANS." Italics indicate Father Delp's underlining, as published in Father Bolkovac's earlier collections of sermons and prison writings.

INTRODUCTION

Advent as a Way of Life

On the first Friday in December 1944, as the Allies were bombing Germany and its defeat was only five months away, a young Jesuit priest was enduring his fifth month of solitary confinement in Berlin. He was awaiting trial for treason for his opposition to Hitler's government. Seated at a rough wooden table in his unheated prison cell, Alfred Delp awkwardly crossed one hand over the other to accommodate his handcuffs as he wrote the words "More, and on a deeper level than before, we really know this time that all of life is Advent" (ADGS 4:36).[1]

Advent had always been one of his favorite subjects. In 1941, his Advent sermons focused on four ways in which Advent "calls" us to an encounter with God:

—we are shaken awake;

—we are called to integrity and authenticity;

—we confess and proclaim our faith;

—we respond to God with reverent awe.

This approach to Advent is what Father Delp called an "Advent of the heart". It is more than preparing ourselves to celebrate the Christmas holiday. It is a spiritual program. It can be a way of life. Father Delp proclaimed that our personal, social, and historical circumstances, even suffering,

[1] The abbreviation ADGS is used for *Alfred Delp: Gesammelte Schriften*, vols. 1–5, ed. Roman Bleistein (Frankfurt am Main, 1982–1984, 1988).

offer us entry into the true Advent, our personal journey toward a meeting and dialogue with God. Indeed, his own life illustrated the true Advent he preached about.

As a Jesuit priest in Munich, Father Delp's artistry lay in taking words from everyday life and giving them a new spiritual interpretation. He appropriated familiar propaganda phrases, which were used to justify war and human-rights violations, and redefined them in a call to truth and social justice. As homes in his parish were shaken by falling bombs, as families were shaken by news of loved ones killed or missing or imprisoned, as an immoral government shook the very foundations of established moral values and human rights, the word "shaking" appeared in Delp's preaching and writing, used as a summons to conversion.

When Alfred Delp entered the Jesuits in 1926, already in motion were social and political events that would lead to World War II and would shape his life and his work as a priest. Long before Delp's priestly ordination in 1937, Hitler had implemented measures to restrict and control the clergy's freedom to speak out on political or moral issues. Preaching against government policies could lead to arrest and imprisonment. Police observers frequently attended religious services in order to report any remark critical of the government. Jesuits were already serving time in prisons and concentration camps. The dangers of political opposition were obvious.

On June 24, 1937, Cardinal Faulhaber ordained Alfred Delp to the priesthood. The front of his ordination card read: "The truth shall make you free" (Jn 8:32). For his motto Delp chose: "No one can lay another foundation than that which has already been laid: Jesus Christ" (1 Cor 3:11). After earning a doctorate in philosophy (1931) and a licentiate in theology (1939), Delp worked for the Jesuit publication

Stimmen der Zeit, and he preached regularly at the Jesuit church of Saint Michæl in Munich.

When the Nazis seized the *Stimmen der Zeit* office buildings and forced the publication to close in 1941, Father Delp was appointed Rector of Saint Georg Church in Munich-Bogenhausen. Delp was considered to be a gripping speaker and took preaching very seriously. He was aware that he was under observation by the Gestapo, so he prepared his sermons meticulously. He discussed potentially dangerous statements with friends beforehand, and he utilized unusual grammatical constructions and vocabulary to give himself a loophole if arrested and questioned. Not only did his listeners understand his message, some took notes in shorthand, typed carbon duplicates, and distributed them to others. Thanks to this practice, more than fifty complete sermon texts were preserved.

Father Delp's personal sense of commitment led him to work with Germany's Resistance movement against Nazism. As a link in an underground referral system assisting Jews who were fleeing the country, he provided food and clothing and directed people to the next hiding place or source of help. In 1942, Count Helmuth James von Moltke (1907–1945) started a Christian Resistance group to plan for the future of Germany after the anticipated defeat of Hitler. This group became known as the Kreisau Circle, named for Moltke's estate, the location of initial meetings. The membership included people of various political, social, and religious backgrounds. They worked together with a particular concern for Germany's cultural, religious, and moral future in the wake of the moral degradation promoted by the Nazis. Delp's Jesuit superior, Provincial Augustin Rösch, S.J., recommended Delp to Moltke as a consultant on Catholic social teachings. Delp also established contacts between the

Kreisau Circle and Catholic members of other Resistance groups.

Moltke was arrested on January 19, 1944, and, without his leadership, the work lost momentum. Some Kreisau members began working with other Resistance groups, including a group of German officers who were planning to assassinate Hitler and take control of the government.

On July 20, 1944, the planned coup failed. A young officer, Claus Schenk von Stauffenberg, planted a bomb in Hitler's meeting room. The bomb exploded, but Hitler survived unharmed, and his appetite for revenge seemed insatiable. Stauffenberg and other officers who had participated in the plot were apprehended and summarily shot the same day. A special Gestapo operation resulted in thousands of arrests and trials for treason. These trials and executions would continue until the end of the war. Members of the Kreisau Circle were arrested and accused of having known of the plot and failing to warn authorities. In this connection, the Gestapo arrested Alfred Delp on July 28, 1944. Like the other "July 20" prisoners, he was interrogated for weeks in a special Gestapo wing of Moabit Prison in Berlin. Despite torture, which he later described as having reduced him to a "bleeding whimper", he did not betray anyone or reveal any useful information.

In mid-August, Delp's friends finally succeeded in learning his location, and they offered him what help they could. Two women from the Resistance movement became responsible for his laundry, using it to smuggle messages, food, and other necessities into his prison cell on a weekly basis. In early September, Delp was transferred to Tegel Prison and the interrogations ended, but he was not formally charged or permitted to meet with an attorney until December. Beginning in October, a sympathetic prison guard helped to supply

Delp with altar bread and small quantities of wine so that he was able to celebrate Mass secretly almost every day.

In accordance with special orders from Hitler's headquarters, prisoners accused of collaborating with the July 20 assassination attempt were kept in solitary confinement and were forced to wear handcuffs constantly as a sign that they were awaiting execution. The prison cells were lighted day and night so the guards could observe the prisoners. Against regulations, and despite the discomfort of his handcuffs, Delp used the glaring light to his advantage and spent many night hours writing. He wrote letters, spiritual meditations, reflections on current social problems, and an account of his trial—all on slips of paper small enough to be concealed and sent out with his laundry.

Father Delp had been scheduled to make his final profession of vows as a Jesuit on August 15, 1944, but his arrest changed everything. During interrogation sessions, the Gestapo repeatedly pressured him to renounce the Jesuits and even promised him his freedom if he would change his allegiance. He refused to do so, but he suffered greatly at the thought that God had not found him worthy to make his final vows. As Advent approached, he prayed a novena with his fellow prisoners, asking to receive at least a small sign of God's grace on the Feast of the Immaculate Conception of Mary, December 8. The dramatic answer to his prayer was the arrival of his friend Father Franz von Tattenbach, who brought the official permission and necessary documents for Father Delp to profess his final vows. Almost overwhelmed with emotion, Alfred Delp pronounced his vows and signed the profession formula with a nervous prison guard at his side. This was the sign of God's love he had waited for, and it renewed his strength for the journey ahead.

After several postponements, Father Delp's trial finally

began on January 9, 1945. Although all charges related to the assassination attempt were dropped, the irreconcilable opposition of Christianity to Nazism became the focus of the proceedings. On January 11, 1945, together with co-defendants Helmuth James von Moltke and Franz Sperr, Alfred Delp was convicted of high treason and sentenced to death by hanging.

Weeks of uncertainty followed the conviction. His co-defendants were executed on January 23, but Father Delp remained in solitary confinement. He and his friends continued to pray and hope for the miracle that would save his life. As the Feast of the Presentation, February 2, approached, Father Delp asked his friends especially to pray for him and emphasized that the feast would fall on the First Friday of February that year. First Friday, a monthly day of devotion to the Sacred Heart of Jesus, had always been special to him.

On Friday afternoon, February 2, 1945, three men were hanged in Plötzensee Prison: Carl Friedrich Goerdeler at 3:19 P.M., Johannes Popitz at 3:21 P.M., and Alfred Delp at 3:23 P.M.[2] Father Franz von Tattenbach later wrote that the Jesuits in Munich had received a number of false reports of Father Delp's execution. When they heard that he had been executed on the Feast of the Presentation, however, they believed it immediately, even before the news could be confirmed. They saw it as a clear and providential sign that God had accepted Father Delp's sacrifice.[3]

[2] According to the records of the German Resistance Memorial Center, Berlin (Dr. Johannes Tuchel, Director, in letter to the translator, October 13, 2004). This date and an afternoon execution time are also supported by Josef Müller, a fellow prisoner who watched guards come to take Goerdeler away to execution (Gerhard Ritter, *Carl Goerdeler und die deutsche Widerstandsbewegung* [Munich: Deutsche Taschenbuch Verlag, 1964], p. 465).

[3] Franz von Tattenbach, "Gefesselte Hände: In Erinnerung an Pater Alfred Delp", in *An unsere Freunde*, January 1951, p. 51.

Parishioners remembered how, on the Feast of the Presentation in 1941, exactly four years before his execution, Father Delp had preached about the symbolism of the blessed candles, which give light at the cost of their own substance. He had spoken prophetically about "comprehending and fulfilling the vocation of a grain of wheat, this call to be poured out extravagantly, to be sacrificed, to give of oneself even unto death, to shine a light from one's very substance for the benefit of others. *Lumen ad revelationem gentium*: Light to enlighten the nations" (ADGS 3:176). Shortly before his execution, Father Delp assured his friends that his life would be "sacrificed, not destroyed". He wrote: "It is the time of sowing, not of harvesting. God is sowing; one day He will harvest again. I will try to do one thing. I will try at least to be a fruitful and healthy seed, falling into the soil. And into the Lord God's hand" (ADGS 4:110).

Alfred Delp's words are not mere abstract idealism. He lived what he preached, and, when his high ideals were tested to the breaking point, he sought and found spiritual meaning in the suffering he endured. First in wartime Munich and, later, from his Berlin prison cell, he preached the timeless spiritual message that we are truly human only when our lives are centered on God. In an extreme situation, Father Delp's faith gave him the courage to live ever closer to God, to witness to the truth even at the cost of his own life, and to put his insights on paper. From the early days of his religious life through the last letters and meditations he wrote from prison, Delp described the season of Advent as a journey into the holy place of encounter with the living God. His words challenge us to embark upon this journey into an "Advent of the heart".

Figures of Advent

More, and on a deeper level than before,
we really know this time
that all of life is Advent.

— Alfred Delp, S.J.
  Letter from prison, December 5, 1944 (ADGS 4:36)

"Figures of Advent"
Written in Tegel Prison, Berlin
December 1944

Advent is a time of being deeply shaken, so that man will wake up to himself.[1] The prerequisite for a fulfilled Advent is a renunciation of the arrogant gestures and tempting dreams with which, and in which, man is always deceiving himself. Thus he compels reality to use violence to bring him around, violence and much distress and suffering.

Being shaken awake is entirely appropriate to thoughts and experiences of Advent. But at the same time there is much more to Advent than this. The shaking is what sets up the secret blessedness of this season and enkindles the inner light in our hearts, so Advent will be blessed with the promises of the Lord. The shaking, the awakening: with these, life merely begins to become capable of Advent. It is precisely in the severity of this awakening, in the helplessness of coming to consciousness, in the wretchedness of experiencing our limitations that the golden threads running between Heaven and earth during this season reach us; the threads that give the world a hint of the abundance to which it is called, the abundance of which it is capable.

Fr. Roman Bleistein's footnotes are translated as they appear in the German text *Alfred Delp: Gesammelte Schriften.* Translator's footnotes and additions to Fr. Bleistein's footnotes are marked "TRANS."

[1] At the time, Luke 21:25–33 was the Gospel for the First Sunday of Advent: "The powers of Heaven will be shaken . . ." (Lk 21:26b). —TRANS.

Man should not grant himself the commonplace, habitual reflections about Advent. He should, however, keep on watching with an inner eye and let his heart roam searchingly. Then he will be able to encounter the earnestness of Advent and the Advent blessing in yet another way. He will see figures, perfected and ideal people of these days and of all time, who personify and live the Advent message and the Advent blessing; and whether cheering or shaking us, consoling or uplifting us, these figures call out and touch mankind. I said, "people of these days and of all time"—primarily, I mean three types: the Voice Calling in the Wilderness, the Angel of Annunciation, and the Blessed Mother.

The Voice Calling in the Wilderness

Blessed is the era that can honestly claim that it is not a desert wilderness.[2] Woe, however, to the era in which the voices calling in the wilderness have fallen silent, shouted down by the noise of the day, or prohibited, or drowned in the intoxication with progress, or restricted and quiet out of fear and cowardice. The devastation will soon take over so horrendously on all sides that the scriptural reference to a *desert wilderness* will spontaneously occur to us all. I think we know this.

Still, the calling voices are not yet raising their lamentation and accusation. Such John the Baptist figures, forged by the lightning of mission and vocation, should never be lacking from life, not for a moment.[3] They are led by their hearts, and that is why their vision is so keen and their judgment is so

[2] In the German, "*Wohl* einer Zeit. . . . *Wehe* aber einer Zeit . . ." parallels Ps 1:1, Mt 5:3, Lk 6:20ff., etc., following old German translations of the Latin Vulgate's *beatus/beati*. —TRANS.

[3] In the preconciliar liturgy, three of the four Advent Sunday Gospels refer to St. John the Baptist. —TRANS.

incorruptible. They do not call for the sake of calling or to hear their own voices. Although they themselves are excluded from the small intimate circle in the foreground, they do not call because they envy man such pleasant earthly hours. They have the great consolation that one can know only after having stepped beyond the deepest and most extreme limits of existence.

They call out blessing and salvation. They call man to face his last chance, because they already feel the ground trembling and the timbers creaking; and they see the steadfast mountains deeply quaking and even the stars of Heaven dangling insecurely. They call man to the potential of averting the spreading wilderness, which is about to fall upon him and crush him, by means of the greater strength of a converted heart.

O God, modern man knows once again in a very practical sense what it means to clear away rubble and to make paths straight again, and he will have to know it and do it for long years to come. May the calling voices indeed ring out, pointing out the wilderness and spiritually overcoming the devastation. May the Advent figure of John the Baptist, of the inexorable messenger and warning prophet in God's name, not be a stranger to our wilderness of ruins. Much in our lives is dependent upon these figures. For how shall we hear if no one calls and the storm of delusion and wild destruction truly overcomes us?

The Angel of Annunciation

I see this year's Advent with an intensity and presentiment like never before. When I pace back and forth in my cell, three steps forward and three steps back, hands in irons, ahead of me an unknown destiny, I understand very differently than before those ancient promises of the coming Lord who will redeem us and set us free. And, along with these thoughts, comes the memory of the angel that a good person gave me for Advent two years ago. It held a banner: "Rejoice, for the Lord is near." A bomb destroyed the angel. A bomb killed the good person, and I often sense that she continues to do angel-services for me.[4] The terror of this time would not be bearable—any more than the terror brought on by our world situation, if we comprehend it—except for this other knowledge that continually encourages us and sets us straight. It is the knowledge of the promises that are being spoken right in the middle of the terror and that are valid.

And it is also knowledge of the quiet angels of annunciation, who speak their message of blessing into the distress and scatter their seeds of the blessing that will begin to grow in the middle of the night. These are not yet the loud angels of public jubilation and fulfillment, these angels of Advent. Silently and unnoticed, they come into private rooms and appear before our hearts as they did long ago. Silently they bring the questions of God and proclaim to us the miracles of God, with whom nothing is impossible.

Advent, despite all earnestness, is a time of refuge because it has received a message. Oh, if people know nothing about the message and the promises anymore, if they only experience the four walls and the prison windows of their gray days, and no longer perceive the quiet footsteps of the announcing angels, if the angels' murmured word does not simultaneously shake us to the depths and lift up our souls— then it is over for us. Then we are living wasted time, and we are dead, long before they do anything to us.

[4] This "good person" might have been Maria Urban, a parishioner who died when her home was hit by a bomb on June 13, 1944 (see "Chronology"). —TRANS.

To believe in the golden seeds of God that the angels have scattered and continue to offer an open heart are the first things we must do with our lives. And the next is to go through these gray days as announcing messengers ourselves. So much courage needs strengthening; so much despair needs comforting; so much hardship needs a gentle hand and an illuminating interpretation; so much loneliness cries out for a liberating word; so much loss and pain seek a spiritual meaning. God's messengers know about the blessing that the Lord God has planted, even within these historic times. To wait in faith, for the fruitfulness of the silent earth and for the abundance of the coming harvest, means to understand the world—even this world—in Advent. To wait in faith—no longer because we trust the earth or the stars or our temperament and good courage—but only because we have perceived God's messages and know about His announcing angels, and even have encountered one.

The Blessed Mother

She is the most comforting figure of Advent. That the angel's message found her heart ready, and the Word became flesh, and in the holy room of her motherly heart the earth grew far beyond its limitations into the human-divine sphere—these are the holiest comforts of Advent. What use to us are the thought and lived experience of our affliction, if no bridge is built to the other shore? How can the terror of chaos and confusion help us, if no light flares up to equal and overcome the darkness? What use to us is this shivering from cold and hardship, in which the world is freezing to death the more it loses and deadens itself deep down inside, if we do not at the same time experience that grace which is mightier than the danger and the lostness?

The poets, and creators of myths, and mankind's other legend- and story-tellers have always spoken of mothers. Sometimes they meant the earth, at other times nature. They wanted to tap into the mysterious, regenerative wellsprings of the universe with this word, and to invoke the outpouring secret of life. In all this there was—and is—hunger, and presentiment, and longing, and an Advent waiting for this blessed woman.

That God would become a mother's son and that a woman could walk upon this earth, her body consecrated as a holy temple and tabernacle for God, is truly the earth's culmination and the fulfillment of its expectation.

The comfort of Advent shines forth in so many various ways from this hidden figure of the blessed and waiting Mary. Oh, that this was granted to the earth, to bring forth such fruit! That the world was permitted to enter into the presence of God through the sheltering warmth, as well as the helpful and reliable patronage of her motherly heart!

The gray horizons must light up. Only the foreground is screaming so loudly and penetratingly. Farther back, where it has to do with things that really count, the situation is already changing. The woman has conceived the Child, sheltered Him under her heart, and has given birth to her Son. The world has come under a different law. All these are not merely one-time historical events upon which our salvation rests. They are simultaneously the model figures and events that announce to us the new order of things, of life, of our existence.

We have to remember courageously today that the blessed woman of Nazareth is one of these illuminating figures. At a deeper level of being, even our times and our destiny bear the blessing and the mystery of God. The most important thing is to wait, to be able to wait, until their hour comes.

Three examples of Advent as a holy, as well as symbolic, figure. This should be no finely drawn idyllic imagery but rather a call addressed to me and to you, dear friend, if these pages find their way to you. It should not so much be nicely said, but rather it should be the truth, against which I measure and align myself and want to keep aligning myself again when the primary burden of these days becomes too heavy and tempts me toward confusion.

Therefore, let us kneel down and pray for the threefold blessing and the threefold consecration of Advent.

Let us pray for the openness and willingness to hear the warning prophets of the Lord and to overcome the devastation of life through conversion of heart. Let us not shun and suppress the earnest words of the calling voices, or those who are our executioners today may be our accusers once again tomorrow, because we silenced the truth.

Once again, let us kneel down and pray for keen eyes capable of seeing God's messengers of annunciation, for vigilant hearts wise enough to perceive the words of the promise. The world is more than its burden, and life is more than the sum of its gray days. The golden threads of the genuine reality are already shining through everywhere. Let us know this, and let us, ourselves, be comforting messengers. Hope grows through the one who is himself a person of the hope and the promise.

One more time, we want to kneel and pray for faith in life's motherly consecration, in the figure of the blessed woman from Nazareth. Already, today and for always, life is torn away from the cruel and merciless powers. Let us be patient and wait, with an Advent waiting for the hour in which it pleases the Lord to appear anew, even in this night, as fruit and mystery of this time.

Advent is the time of the promise, not yet the fulfillment.

We are still standing in the middle of the whole thing, in the logical relentlessness and inevitability of destiny. To captive eyes,[5] it still appears that the ultimate throw of the dice indeed will be cast here below in these valleys, on these battlefields, in these camps, and prisons, and cellars. One keeping vigil, though, senses the other powers at work and can await their hour.

The sounds of devastation and destruction, the cries of self-importance and arrogance, the weeping of despair and powerlessness still fill the world. Yet, standing silently, all along the horizon are the eternal realities with their age-old longing. The first gentle light of the glorious abundance to come is already shining above them. From out there, the first sounds are ringing out like shepherds' flutes and a boys' choir singing. They do not yet form a song or melody—it is all still too far off and only the first announcement and intimation. Still, it is happening. This is today. And tomorrow the angels will relate loudly and jubilantly what has happened, and we will know it and will be blessed if we have believed and trusted in Advent.

[5] The German expression *gehaltene Augen* literally means "held eyes", that is, eyes that are prevented from perceiving the truth. In the Latin Vulgate and in many German Bible translations, the disciples on the road to Emmaus are described as having "held eyes" that therefore did not recognize Jesus (see Lk 24:16). —TRANS.

Week I

Advent means
a heart that is awake and ready.

— Alfred Delp, S.J.
  Advent Holy Hour, 1942

Liturgy for the First Sunday of Advent

Introit: Psalm 25(24):1–4

Ad te levavi animam meam: Deus meus, in te confido, non erubescam: neque irrideant me inimici mei: etenim universi, qui te exspectant, non confundentur. Vias tuas, Domine, demonstra mihi: et semitas tuas edoce me. Gloria Patri, et Filio, et Spiritui Sancto. Sicut erat in principio, et nunc, et semper, et in sæcula sæculorum. Amen.

To You I lift up my soul. My God, I trust in You. Do not let me be put to shame, nor let my enemies mock me, for those who wait for You will not be disappointed. Show me Your ways, O Lord, and teach me Your paths. Glory be to the Father, and to the Son, and to the Holy Spirit. As it was in the beginning, is now, and ever shall be, world without end. Amen.

Collect:

Excita, quæsumus, Domine, potentiam tuam, et veni: ut ab imminentibus peccatorum nostrorum periculis, te mereamur protegente eripi, te liberante salvari: Qui vivis et regnas cum Deo Patre in unitate Spiritus Sancti, Deus, per omnia sæcula sæculorum. Amen.

Awaken Your power, we beseech You, O Lord, and come. Then we will be rescued by Your protection and saving action from the dangers that threaten us because of our sin. You who live and reign with God the Father in the unity of the Holy Spirit, God, for ever and ever. Amen.

Epistle: Romans 13:11–14

Fratres: Scientes, quia hora est jam nos de somno surgere. Nunc enim propior est nostra salus, quam cum credidimus. Nox præcessit, dies autem appropinquavit. Abjiciamus ergo opera tenebrarum, et induamur arma lucis. Sicut in die honeste ambulemus: non in comessationibus, et ebrietatibus, non in cubilibus, et impudicitiis, non in contentione, et æmulatione: sed induimini Dominum Jesum Christum.

Brethren: You know the hour has come to arise from sleep, because now our salvation is nearer than before, when we came to believe. The night is far advanced; the day is near. Let us therefore lay aside the works of darkness, and put on the weapons of light. Let us walk honorably as in the daytime, not in indulgence and drinking bouts, not in lewdness and debauchery, not in contention and jealousy. Instead, put on the Lord Jesus Christ.

Gradual: Psalm 25(24):3–4

Universi, qui te exspectant, non confundentur Domine.
V. Vias tuas Domine notas fac mihi: et semitas tuas edoce me.

Those who wait for You will not be disappointed, O Lord.
V. Show me Your ways, O Lord, and teach me Your paths.

Alleluia: Psalm 85(84):8

Alleluia, alleluia.
V. Ostende nobis, Domine, misericordiam tuam: et salutare tuum da nobis. Alleluia.

Alleluia, alleluia.
V. Show us, O Lord, Your mercy, and grant us Your salvation. Alleluia.

Gospel: Luke 21:25–33

In illo tempore: Dixit Jesus discipulis suis: Erunt signa in sole, et luna, et stellis, et in terris pressura gentium præ confusione sonitus maris, et fluctuum: arescentibus hominibus præ timore, et exspectatione, quæ supervenient universo orbi: nam virtutes cælorum movebuntur. Et tunc videbunt Filium hominis venientem in nube cum potestate magna, et majestate. His autem fieri incipientibus, respicite, et levate capita vestra: quoniam appropinquat redemptio vestra. Et dixit illis similitudinem: Videte ficulneam, et omnes arbores: cum producunt jam ex se fructum, scitis quoniam prope est æstas. Ita et vos cum videritis hæc fieri, scitote quoniam prope est regnum Dei. Amen dico vobis, quia non præteribit generatio hæc, donec omnia fiant. Cælum, et terra transibunt: verba autem mea non transibunt.

At that time, Jesus said to His disciples: "Signs will appear in the sun, moon, and stars, and upon the earth there will be great anxiety among the peoples because of the turbulent rushing of seas and rivers. The people will languish in fearful expectation as they await the things that will come over the entire world; for the powers of Heaven will be shaken. Then they will see the Son of Man coming upon the clouds with great power and glory. When these things begin to come to pass, look up, and lift up your heads, because your redemption is near." He told them a parable: "Observe the fig tree and all the other trees. When they bear fruit, you know that the summer is near. In the same way, when all these things happen, you should know that the Kingdom of God is near. Truly, I say to you, this generation will not pass away until all of this happens. Heaven and earth will pass away, but My words will not pass away."

Offertory: Psalm 25(24):1–3

Ad te levavi animam meam: Deus meus, in te confido, non erubescam: neque irrideant me inimici mei: etenim universi, qui te exspectant, non confundentur.

To You I lift up my soul. My God, I trust in You, I will not be put to shame, nor will my enemies mock me. Those who wait for You will not be disappointed.

Secret:

Hæc sacra nos, Domine, potenti virtute mundatos ad suum faciant puriores venire principium. Per Dominum nostrum Jesum Christum, Filium tuum, qui tecum vivit et regnat in unitate Spiritus Sancti, Deus, per omnia sæcula sæculorum. Amen.

O Lord, may these holy gifts purify us through their mighty strength, and make us capable, totally pure, to approach Him who is their source. Through our Lord Jesus Christ, Your Son, who lives and reigns with You in the unity of the Holy Spirit, God, for ever and ever. Amen.

Communion: Psalm 85(84):13

Dominus dabit benignitatem et terra nostra dabit fructum suum.

The Lord will give goodness and our earth will give its fruit.

Postcommunion:

Suscipiamus, Domine, misericordiam tuam in medio templi tui: ut reparationis nostræ ventura solemnia congruis honoribus præcedamus. Per Dominum nostrum Jesum Christum, Filium tuum, qui tecum

vivit et regnat in unitate Spiritus Sancti, Deus, per omnia sæcula
sæculorum. Amen.

Lord, in the midst of Your temple may we receive Your
mercy within us, so that we may prepare ourselves with
appropriate reverence for this coming feast of our redemption. Through our Lord Jesus Christ, Your Son, who lives
and reigns with You in the unity of the Holy Spirit, God, for
ever and ever. Amen.

Homily for the First Sunday of Advent
Preached in Munich
November 30, 1941

"Those who wait for you will not be disappointed" (Ps 25:3). Somehow unaffected by all that has happened in the course of one year, somehow untouched by all the great and all the small, all the lovely and all the loathsome things that, in the course of one year, might affect the earth, on this first Sunday in Advent the Church gives voice to her ancient prayer: "Ad te levavi animam meam"—"To You I lift up my soul." And, wherever they are still allowed to express the idea of this day as they wish, the people give voice to traditional Advent hymns.[1] Letting go of our concerns about all that we are going through in our lives, we recognize this one thing: the season of Advent is a time with its own special access to our hearts, its own special access to our souls and minds. This season is more to us than just remembering devout, blessed childhood days, when we awaited the great and happy holiday and spiritually prepared ourselves.

The spiritual preparation is still there for all those who have eyes at all, who have ears at all, and who are listening and watching with their minds, hearts, and souls for the things dealt with here. The main point of Advent is not merely to

---

[1] Fr. Delp named two well-known German Advent hymns: "Tauet, Himmel, den Gerechten" and "O Heiland, reiß den Himmel auf". He mentioned the same two hymns in his 1933 Advent play, *The Eternal Advent* (see Appendix II). —Trans.

remember and reenact some kind of historical waiting. No, Advent centers on fundamental principles and fundamental attitudes of our lives, of life in general, and of existence in general. These will be presented in the context of historical waiting, physically and visibly, while being modified like a motif. This motif will be visualized, actualized, and thought through in a new way—and prayed over in a new way as well. That is the very deepest meaning of Advent. Our holy seasons always ought to be something special. They are really holy mysteries, and they should awaken a mystery as echo, as consideration, as prayer, in our minds and in our hearts.

The theme of this Advent is that, somehow, man will be confronted with the Last Things, will be placed in the final order, will face the definitive questions, and definitive answers will be expected of him.[2] Whenever the Church dons solemn purple vestments, it always means that serious questions are being set forth and we are facing the great connections, the principles of universal validity. Indeed, after all, the ultimate and deepest meaning of this coming feast, this Christmas and Coming-of-the-Lord for which we are preparing ourselves, is that the created being, man, actually finds himself in the presence of the Absolute Ultimate. Moreover, the basic readying of our souls for this feast of the coming Lord is that we now consider the ultimate reality. This means that we think about man, about ourselves, from the perspective of the ultimate reality and, in so doing, become ready—really ready—to encounter and respond to Him, the Ultimate, in an appropriate way, as befits a creature encountering the Ultimate. It means really being ready to meet Him

[2] The term "Last Things" refers to death, particular judgment, Heaven, Hell, Purgatory, the Second Coming of Christ, the resurrection of the dead, the General Judgment, the end of the world, and the establishment of God's Kingdom. —TRANS.

in this way. Therefore, that should be our theme for these
Advent reflections: man from the perspective of the ultimate
reality; what ultimately is, and what ultimately will be. The
ultimate reality cannot be affected in any way by any whirlwind, any turmoil, any arrogance or hubris. It cannot be
shaken in its own validity, and, when it is tampered with,
those raising a hand or fist against it only affect themselves.[3]

The liturgy introduces man to the end through statements
and instruction. The first thing the liturgy emphasizes and
tries to evoke in us through this encounter with the end is a
shaking. In today's Gospel, once again we hear the message of
the last days of the world, briefly summarized and compact,
compressed together into this one point: *everything will be
shaken*. "There will be signs appearing in the sun, moon, and
stars. Great anxiety will be among the people because of the
violent rushing of seas and rivers. The people will languish in
fearful expectation of the things that will come over the
entire face of the earth. The powers of Heaven will be
shaken. And then they will see the Son of Man coming on
the clouds with great might and glory. Now when all of this
begins, then look up and raise your heads, for your redemption is near" (Lk 21:25–28). This tells us one thing. Here, in
the shaking of the world, when the foundations are collaps-
ing, then lift up your heads because your redemption is drawing near. The Son of Man will come.

Saint Paul's Epistle to the Romans expresses something
similar, but approaches it from the ethical sphere: "Brothers,
you know the hour has come to arise from sleep, because
now our salvation is nearer than before, when we began to
believe. The night is far advanced; the day is breaking. Let us
lay aside the works of darkness and put on the weapons of

[3] In 1941, the raised hand and the raised fist were two salutes used by
supporters of totalitarian regimes. —TRANS.

light. Let us walk honorably as in the daytime. . . . Put on the Lord Jesus Christ" (Rom 13:11-14). This depicts personal redemption as the experience of being shaken, being awakened, becoming sober, and being transformed; personal redemption as an experience of preparing to go from night into the day.

In the Opening Prayer, we prayed: "Awaken Your power, we beseech You, O Lord, and come. Then we will be rescued by Your protection and saving action from the dangers that threaten us because of our sin. You who live and reign with God the Father in the unity of the Holy Spirit, God, for ever and ever." Again, salvation; redemption; encounter with the Lord; a rescue from being threatened, from being insecure, from being shaken, from being in danger.

Perhaps what we modern people need most is to be genuinely shaken, so that where life is grounded, we would feel its stability; and where life is unstable and uncertain, immoral and unprincipled, we would know that, also, and endure it. Perhaps that is the ultimate answer to the question of why God has sent us into this time, why He permits this whirlwind to go over the earth, and why He holds us in such a state of chaos and in hopelessness and in darkness—and why there is no end in sight. It is because we have stood here on the earth with a totally false and inauthentic sense of security. So now, God lets the earth resound, and now He shudders it, and then He shakes it, not to call forth a false anxiety—I will speak of that later. He does it to teach us one thing again: how to be moved in spirit. Much of what is happening today would not be happening if people were in that state of inner movement and restlessness of heart in which man comes into the presence of God the Lord and gains a clear view of things as they really are. Then man would have let go of much that has thrown all our lives into disorder one way or another and has thrashed and smashed our lives. He would have seen the inner appeals, would have seen the boundaries, and could have coordinated the areas of responsibility. Instead, man stood on this earth in a false pathos and a false security, under a deep delusion in which he really believed he could single-handedly fetch stars from heaven; could enkindle eternal lights in the world and avert all danger from himself; that he could banish the night, and intercept and interrupt the internal quaking of the cosmos, and maneuver and manipulate the whole thing into the conditions standing before us now.

That is the first Advent message: before the end, the world will be set quaking. And only where man does not cling inwardly to false security will his eyes be capable of seeing the Ultimate. Only then will he get down to basics and preserve himself and his life from these pedagogical terrors and horrors into which God the Lord must let the world sink, so that we—as Saint Paul said—will awaken from sleep and see that it is just about time to turn around. It is just about time to change things. It is just about time to say: Fine, it was night, but let the night pass, and let us decide now for day. Let us decide with a determination that comes directly out of these terrifying experiences, out of these lived connections, and that is therefore completely unshakable, even in the midst of instability.

If we want to transform life once more, and if it really ought to become Advent once more—Advent of the homeland, and Advent of hearts, and Advent of our people, and Advent of all peoples—and, included in all that, the coming of the Lord—then the one great Advent question for us is whether we can come out of these shakings with the resolve: Yes, arise! It is time to awaken from sleep. It is time for an awakening to begin somewhere; and it is time that someone places things again in the order that they were given by God the Lord. Moreover, now it is time for each individual to use every opportunity to guide life into this order now—and to do it with the same "unshakeability" with which the Lord will come. Where life heeds your word, you must not misrepresent the message. Where life rebels before your very eyes, you must set it right. These days life lacks people who can come through the final shakings—as well as through these present shakings—with the knowledge and the consciousness: those who are watching for the Lord will not be affected, in the eternal sense, even if they are hunted off the face of the earth.

Homily for the First Sunday of Advent
Preached in Munich
November 28, 1943

"Those who wait for You will not be disappointed" (Ps 25:3). Despite this gloomy time, with a certitude about life and faith, we have set up the Advent wreath, even though no one knows how long it will stand or whether all four of its candles will be lit. The course of the liturgical year and the message continues, and we keep on doing things—but not for the sake of custom and tradition. It comes from a sense of certitude about things and mankind and revelation—things that are fixed and valid in and of themselves. These give mankind the right to light candles and to believe in the light and brightness of existence. Not as if it were granted to us to erase all the gloominess! All the gloom must be gone through and endured. Yet, precisely for that reason, the lights of Advent should shine forth from within as we let ourselves be led to the insight that man is not under a law of imprisonment, enslavement, threats.[1]

Advent is similar to the time before Easter. When we go forth toward the great mysteries, we should consider the proper order of our lives in the weeks beforehand. Ahead of

[1] Compare Rom 8:2, 15: "For the law of the Spirit of life in Christ Jesus has set you free from the law of sin and of death. For you did not receive the spirit of slavery to fall back into fear, but you have received the spirit of sonship." —TRANS.

time, from a distance, we should review our lives and take a
sober look at things because reality is still the place where
true joy grows and where we build things that can support a
load.

The message of the First Sunday of Advent is to attain to
the source. It is a Sunday whose basic insight gives a particular
expression to the objectivity of our existence. It enlightens
our lives and dismisses what is questionable, so that we can
believe in the brightness. Man must learn once again that the
fundamental character of this time is not one of activity.
Occidentals, increasingly busy, seeking to have and to possess,
easily gamble away the meaning. Man must realize that he is
a wayfarer, a scout, hungering and restless. He is dependent
upon an angel approaching and touching him with the wing-
stroke reminder of a higher message.

Even so, our waiting is not the end. In today's Gospel
about the end of the world, we read: "The people will languish in fearful expectation as they await the things that will
come over the entire world; for the powers of Heaven will be
shaken" (Lk 21:26). There is a character of fearful expectation when things start to tremble, when life is felt to be so
menacing. Nevertheless, it is bourgeois simply to wait for the
sky to become light again. This experience of waiting will
continue to be wrongly understood unless one sees that we
are meant to learn from it. Man is not permitted to fixate
himself too much within his own sphere of life, settling
himself too firmly in place until he is chased away. We will
wrongly understand this waiting if we forget that the deeper
meaning of life is to keep watch.

Here is what lies behind it: man must notice and feel that
the longing for sun, for happiness, is only the foreground;
that it is his affliction to hunger for something more; that he
is not really human until the good is actualized before him

and love is activated within him. There is no earthly event, power, or love that can bring peace to man's heart. There are promises about mankind: above and beyond all your wishes and ideas, what counts is that the Lord has consecrated and created you for an intimacy with God that "no human eye has seen, no human ear has heard" (1 Cor 2:9). We are designed for this. We also need to ask the question, "Why is it like this?"

There is nothing more blessed in life than true waiting, but there is also no greater *un*-blessedness than "having to wait", for each plan is thwarted and left in fragments. Why is it this way? You must reach out, but you will not essentially get beyond yourself if the Other does not come to meet you. Man is truly human only when he transcends himself. He becomes small when he is content with things and values from his own life sphere. For this reason, he feels a sense of annoyance when fulfillment does not happen, since he still has the vague sense that values once dwelt among mankind. But then confusion entered in, and reality slipped from our fingers. Individuals, like mankind in general, keep falling into mental weariness—what is more, into the diabolical. This is why the Lord calls each one of us to this awakening, to this self-reflection. The liturgy today should not just mean pious words to us, but, in these difficult times, this should become a season of reflection. We should discover life and its fundamental order.

This should be our first Advent light: to understand everything, all that happens to us and all that threatens us, from the perspective of life's character of waiting. We must endure all the blessedness and *un*-blessedness of waiting because we are under way. The character of life is to keep going, to keep a lookout, and to endure until the vigilant heart of man and the heart of God who meets us come together: presently in

the true interior meeting in the sacraments and, later, in the
final homecoming. God enters only His own rooms, where
someone is always keeping watch for Him. Indeed—like all
other things in another sense that the Lord will add unto
us[2]—we will experience again: "Those who really wait for
Him will not be disappointed."

People who fail to live out of the center can be alienated
from themselves so easily by outside influences. Other values
of secondary importance impose themselves, making life inauthentic and bringing it under an alien law and an alien
paradigm. Are we living out of the center of our being, or
from memory, from impulses, but not because we are settled
in the center of reality and find our stability nourished there?
This is the deeper sense of Advent: that we scrutinize this
center, little by little, and set up lights of recognition in our
lives, and, from the center, master life's gloominess. There is
no absolute darkness. We just have to seek truly and to reach
out. People who do not live out of the center will be alienated easily by outside influences, but those who really wait on
the Lord God will not be disappointed.

There are two messages today: first, we have to hold on to
absolute responsibility for real order and commitment to the
Lord God. Second, the fundamental character of life is a true
waiting, hard for Occidentals to comprehend, especially for
modern people. Life means waiting, not Faust-like grasping,
but waiting and being ready. We are waiting for the terror of
the night, and waiting for the day when this terror will have
passed. "The people will languish from fearful expectation."
Anyone who remains stuck, waiting in fearful expectation
just to see whether or not he will survive, has not yet laid bare

[2] Compare Lk 12:29 and 31: "Do not worry about what you are to eat and
what you are to wear. . . . Seek the Kingdom of God first, and all these things
shall be added to you as well." —TRANS.

the innermost strata. For the fearful expectation was sent to us in order to remove our false sense of security, and behind it is this other metaphysical waiting that is part of existence. Man is always in danger of rooting himself, of running aground. Over and over again, life will shake anyone who only waits in that way, in order to make him hurry out to meet what is coming. Then what vitality he has been given will come to life. Then he will feel that life goes above and beyond individual lives. Only in this way will he be truly human, by living above and beyond himself, waiting for the final reality. That is the reason for this striving and seeking further and knowing it will one day come: to wait until the lights flare up.

We have more expectation than earth can grant, because what we encounter is only a piece of reality, a piece of creation. We are waiting for the fulfillment of a promise: You will one day possess all this because God, as God, is Himself reality, realness, and intimacy. Still, we must be careful not to revert to childish naïveté. Often a pure feeling of annoyance comes over us due to the order of our present reality. We resent always having to run around hungry. A long time ago, something went off the track. Since then, man has had to endure the hunger for fulfillment. We must remain in the real Advent; we should not harden ourselves, not capitulate from horror or from happiness, but keep the authentic attitude of waiting because we know: we are going out to meet a Goodness, a Benevolence.

However, having to wait means that one is in danger of mental weariness. Therefore, today's Epistle offers the encouragement: "The hour has come to arise from sleep" (Rom 13:11). Take your head in hand, so to speak, and examine yourself as you are. Measure yourself against the great scale to see whether you are alienated by outside influences, or are still rooted in the source of strength. Perhaps you are saying, "What's the use?" If you enter into this reflection, you will be rejuvenated and connected with the source. Then these jolts will not always be necessary. Then that source will well up within you, like an interior stream flowing and carrying you onward. Now it begins: *Those who genuinely wait on the Lord God will not be disappointed.* They will grow into this true meeting with God, an encounter in mystery and in grace. It all depends upon our waiting, staying vigilant, and straining toward what lies ahead with a true openness.

Meditation for the First Sunday of Advent
Written in Tegel Prison, Berlin
December 1944

The deepest meaning of Advent cannot be understood by anyone who has not first experienced being terrified unto death about himself and his human prospects and likewise what is revealed within himself about the situation and constitution of mankind in general.[1]

This entire message about God's coming, about the Day of Salvation, about redemption drawing near, will be merely

---

[1] It appears that Fr. Delp may be referring to Martin Luther's statement in his commentary on the Seven Penitential Psalms. Delp uses the words "*zu Tode erschrocken*", here translated as "terrified unto death". In comparison, Luther's comment on Ps 6:4, "My soul is struck with terror [*ist sehr erschrocken*]", reads: "God's strength and consolation are given to no one unless he asks for it from the bottom of his heart. But no one who has not been profoundly terrified [*gründlich erschrocken*] and forsaken prays profoundly" (J. Pelikan and H. T. Lehman, eds., *Luther's Works*, American edition [St. Louis: Concordia Publishing House, 1958–1986], 14:141).

It seems feasible that Tegel Prison's Lutheran chaplain, who often visited Fr. Delp, might have encouraged him with these very words.

Luther's words are probably more familiar in Germany than in the English-speaking countries. For example, in an interview with Peter Seewald, Pope Benedict XVI, then Cardinal Ratzinger, recalled the same passage as follows: "But we need to be frightened [*erschrocken*] of ourselves and out of our self-complacency. Here, I think, Luther was right when he said that man must first be frightened [*erschrocken*] of himself, so that he can then find the right way" (Joseph Cardinal Ratzinger, *Salt of the Earth* [San Francisco: Ignatius Press, 1997], p. 26). —TRANS.

divine game-playing or sentimental lyricism unless it is grounded upon two clear findings of fact.

The first finding: insight into, and alarm over the power-lessness and futility of human life in relation to its ultimate meaning and fulfillment. The powerlessness and futility are both boundaries of our existence and are also consequences of sin. At the same time, we are keenly aware that life does have an ultimate meaning and fulfillment.

The second finding: the promise of God to be on our side, to come to meet us. God resolved to raise the boundaries of our existence and to overcome the consequences of sin.

However, as a result, the basic condition of life always has an Advent dimension: boundaries, and hunger, and thirst, and lack of fulfillment, and promise, and movement toward one another. That means, however, that we basically remain without shelter, under way, and open until the final encoun-ter, with all the humble blessedness and painful pleasure of this openness.

Therefore there is no interim finality, and the attempt to create final conclusions is an old temptation of mankind. Hunger and thirst, and desert journeying, and the survival teamwork of mountaineers on a rope—these are the truth of our human condition. The promises given relate to this truth, not to arrogance and caprice. There really are promises given to this truth though, and we can and should rely upon them. *The truth will make you free* (Jn 8:32).[2]

That truth is the essential theme of life. Everything else is only expression, result, application, consequence, testing, and practice. May God help us to wake up to ourselves and in doing so, to move from ourselves toward Him.

Every temptation to live according to other conditions is a

[2] Fr. Delp had this verse printed on the front of his ordination card in 1937. —TRANS.

deception. Our participation in this existential lie is really the sin for which we today—as individuals, as a generation, and as a continent—are so horribly doing penance. The way to salvation will be found only in an existential conversion and return to the truth.

This is, however, a conversion and a return that allow for no procrastination. "Ab imminentibus peccatorum . . . periculis! [The dangers that threaten us because of sin!]"[3] The existential untruth and continuing entanglement in it are not matters left to personal discretion. The lie is dangerously destructive. It has corroded our souls, destroyed our people, demolished our cities and countries, and already has let yet another generation bleed to death.

"Universi, qui te exspectant, non confundentur [Those who wait for You will not be disappointed]."[4] May we know and acknowledge the hunger and thirst above and beyond ourselves. Indeed, this is no waiting without hope. Rather, the heart receives the delightful warmth known to those who wait with the certitude that the other is coming and has already set out on the way.

The terror that accompanies such an awakening to one's own situation is finally and conclusively overcome from within by the certitude that God has already set out and is on His way. Our destinies, still so interwoven with the inescapable "logical" and "mechanical" course of events, are really nothing other than the ways that God the Lord uses to bring about this definitive meeting, as well as His ongoing inquiry. "Levate capita vestra: quoniam appropinquat redemptio vestra [Lift up your heads: Your salvation is near]" (Lk 21:28).

In the same way that lies have gone out from people's hearts, penetrating throughout the world and destroying it,

---

[3] Liturgy: Collect for the First Sunday of Advent.
[4] Gradual for First Sunday of Advent, Ps 25(24):3.

so should—and so will—the truth begin its healing service within our hearts.

Light the candles wherever you can, you who have them. They are a real symbol of what must happen in Advent, what Advent must be, if we want to live.[5]

[5] Fr. Delp spoke in detail about candles as a symbol in his February 2, 1941, sermon: "This is a peaceful, reticent, but constant shining. This is giving light at the cost of one's own substance, so that one is consumed in the process. Anyone who wants to comprehend Christ's message of light . . . must comprehend this one thing: the mission, the duty to shine, to draw others, to seek, to heal, to do good at the cost of one's own substance . . ." (ADGS, 3:175). —TRANS.

Week II

Our hearts must be keenly alert for opportunities in our own little corners of daily life. May we stand in this world, not as people in hiding, but as those who help prepare the way of the only-begotten Son of God.

— Alfred Delp, S.J.
  Second Sunday of Advent, 1942

Liturgy for the Second Sunday of Advent

Introit: Isaiah 30:30, Psalm 80(79):2

Populus Sion, ecce Dominus veniet ad salvandas gentes: et auditam faciet Dominus gloriam vocis suæ in lætitia cordis vestri. Qui regis Israël, intende: qui deducis, velut ovem, Joseph. Gloria Patri, et Filio, et Spiritui Sancto. Sicut erat in principio, et nunc, et semper, et in sæcula sæculorum. Amen.

People of Zion, see, the Lord will come to redeem the nations and the Lord will let His glorious word be heard, giving joy to your hearts. Attend, you shepherds of Israel, you who lead Joseph like a sheep. Glory be to the Father, and to the Son, and to the Holy Spirit. As it was in the beginning, is now, and ever shall be, world without end. Amen.

Collect:

Excita, Domine, corda nostra ad præparandas Unigeniti tui vias: ut, per ejus adventum, purificatis tibi mentibus servire mereamur. Qui tecum vivit et regnat in unitate Spiritus Sancti, Deus, per omnia sæcula sæculorum. Amen.

Awaken our hearts, O Lord, to prepare the way for Your only-begotten Son, that we may serve You with minds that are purified through His coming, who lives and reigns with You in the unity of the Holy Spirit, God, for ever and ever. Amen.

Epistle: Romans 15:4–13

Fratres: Quæcumque scripta sunt, ad nostram doctrinam scripta sunt: ut per patientiam et consolationem Scripturarum spem habeamus. Deus autem patientiæ et solatii det vobis idipsum sapere in alterutrum secundum Jesum Christum: ut unanimes, uno ore honorificetis Deum et Patrem Domini nostri Jesu Christi. Propter quod suscipite invicem, sicut et Christus suscepit vos in honorem Dei. Dico enim Christum Jesum ministrum fuisse circumcisionis propter veritatem Dei, ad confirmandas promissiones patrum: gentes autem super misericordia honorare Deum, sicut scriptum est: Propterea confitebor tibi in gentibus, Domine, et nomini tuo cantabo. Et iterum dicit: Lætamini, gentes, cum plebe ejus. Et iterum: Laudate, omnes gentes, Dominum: et magnificate eum, omnes populi. Et rursus Isaias ait: Erit radix Jesse, et qui exsurget regere gentes, in eum gentes sperabunt. Deus autem spei repleat vos omni gaudio et pace in credendo: ut abundetis in spe et virtute Spiritus Sancti.

Brethren: Everything that is written was written for our learning, so that, through the patience and comfort given by the Scriptures, we might have hope. The God of patience and comfort grant you to be of one mind among each other, according to Christ Jesus, so that with one mind and one mouth, God the Father of our Lord Jesus Christ may be glorified. Therefore, accept one another, as Christ has accepted you, for the honor of God. For I say to you, Christ Jesus is the servant of the circumcision for the truth of God, to fulfill the promises given to our fathers. The other nations, however, are to glorify God in His mercy, as it is written, "Therefore I will praise You among the nations, O Lord, and will sing to Your name." And again, it is said, "Rejoice, you nations, with His people." And again, "Praise the Lord, all you nations, magnify Him, all you peoples." And Isaiah said,

"A root will come from Jesse, and He shall rise up to rule over the nations, in Him the nations will hope." Now the God of hope fill you with all joy and peace through the faith, that you may overflow with hope and the power of the Holy Spirit.

Gradual: Psalm 50(49):2–3, 5

Ex Sion species decoris ejus. Deus manifeste veniet.
V. Congregate illi sanctos ejus, qui ordinaverunt testamentum ejus super sacrificia.

The loveliness of His beauty shall shine from Zion. God shall come and manifest Himself.
V. Gather His saints together, who have preferred His covenant to sacrifices.

Alleluia: Psalm 122(121):1

Alleluia, alleluia.
V. Lætatus sum in his, quæ dicta sunt mihi: in domum Domini ibimus. Alleluia.

Alleluia, alleluia.
V. I rejoiced as they said to me, let us go to the house of the Lord. Alleluia.

Gospel: Matthew 11:2–10

In illo tempore: Cum audisset Joannes in vinculis opera Christi, mittens duos de discipulis suis, ait illi:Tu es, qui venturus es, an alium expectamus? Et respondens Jesus, ait illis: Euntes renuntiate Joanni, quæ audistis et vidistis. Cæci vident, claudi ambulant, leprosi mundantur, surdi audiunt, mortui resurgunt, pauperes evangelizantur:

et beatus est, qui non fuerit scandalizatus in me. Illis autem abeun-
tibus, coepit Jesus dicere ad turbas de Joanne: Quid existis in
desertum videre? arundinem vento agitatam? Sed quid existis videre?
hominem mollibus vestitum? Ecce, qui mollibus vestiuntur, in
domibus regum sunt. Sed quid existis videre? prophetam? Etiam dico
vobis, et plus quam prophetam. Hic est enim, de quo scriptum est:
Ecce, ego mitto Angelum meum ante faciem tuam, qui præparabit
viam tuam ante te.

At that time, as John, in chains, heard of the works of
Christ, he sent two of his disciples asking, "Are You the one
who is to come, or should we look for another?" Jesus
answered them, saying, "Go and tell John what you have
heard and seen. The blind see, the lame walk, lepers are
cleansed, the deaf hear, the dead are raised to life, the poor
are evangelized, and blessed is he who does not take offense
at me." After they had gone, Jesus spoke to the people about
John: "What did you go out into the desert to see? A reed
driven to and fro by the wind? Or what did you go out to
see? A man in soft clothing? Look, those wearing soft clothing are in the palaces of kings. Or why did you go out?
What did you want to see? A prophet? Yes, I say to you, and
more than a prophet. This is the one of whom it is written,
'See, I send my messenger before You to prepare the way for
You.'"

Offertory: Psalm 85(84):7-8

Deus, tu conversus vivificabis nos, et plebs tua lætabitur in te: ostende
nobis, Domine, misericordiam tuam, et salutare tuum da nobis.

God, turn toward us and give us new life, then Your people
will rejoice in You. Show us Your mercy, O Lord, and grant
us Your salvation.

Secret:

Placare quæsumus, Domine, humilitatis nostræ precibus et hostiis: et ubi nulla suppetunt suffragia meritorum, tuis nobis succurre præsidiis. Per Dominum nostrum Jesum Christum, Filium tuum, qui tecum vivit et regnat in unitate Spiritus Sancti, Deus, per omnia sæcula sæculorum. Amen.

We beseech You, O Lord, be appeased by our humble prayers and offerings and where our own merits are lacking, grant us the aid of Your protection. Through our Lord Jesus Christ, Your Son, who lives and reigns with You in the unity of the Holy Spirit, God, for ever and ever. Amen.

Communion: Baruch 5:5, 4:36

Jerusalem, surge, et sta in excelso, et vide jucunditatem, quæ veniet tibi a Deo tuo.

Jerusalem, rise up and stand on high, and see the joy that is coming to you from your God.

Postcommunion:

Repleti cibo spiritualis alimoniæ, supplices te, Domine, deprecamur: ut, hujus participatione mysterii, doceas nos terrena despicere et amare cælestia. Per Dominum nostrum Jesum Christum, Filium tuum, qui tecum vivit et regnat in unitate Spiritus Sancti, Deus, per omnia sæcula sæculorum. Amen.

Filled through receiving Your spiritual nourishment, we beseech You, O Lord: teach us through our participation in these mysteries to reject earthly goods and to love heavenly things. Through our Lord Jesus Christ, Your Son, who lives and reigns with You in the unity of the Holy Spirit, God, for ever and ever. Amen.

Homily for the Second Sunday of Advent Preached in Munich December 7, 1941

"Why did you go out into the desert? What did you want to see?" (Mt 11:7). We spoke last Sunday about how, for us, Advent is more than the celebration of some kind of historical remembrance, and more than the celebration of a season with its own liturgical color and its own liturgical ritual. Each liturgical season has its own individual meaning and its own assignment. In that sense, the deepest meaning of Advent is man's meeting with the Ultimate, with the Absolute. Therefore, our Advent considerations comprised man's understanding in perspective of the end, man encountering the Absolute with the knowledge of the end, the final destination. We considered what will become of us there and how we should inwardly, on the deepest level, decide and live and act from this spiritual center and prove ourselves.

The first Advent message about this encounter with the Absolute, with the end, was the Gospel message that we read last Sunday about the violent shaking. At the end, the world will be shaken; and then the Son of Man will come. That is more than just historical prophecy. It is also a basic principle that somehow the coming of God and the shaking of mankind are connected. It means that then, if man is inwardly unshaken, inwardly incapable of a real deep shaking—if he continues to be obstinate and hard and superficial and inadequate—then God the Lord will intervene in world history

Himself. He will teach us what it means to be set shaking and to be touched at the very center of our being. Therefore, the big question for us is whether we are still capable of truly being shaken, or shall it continue this way? Shall it continue that we look at thousands and thousands of things and know about them? That we know about those things that we don't like—about things which we know should not be and must not be—and that we accustom ourselves to all of it? What have we already accustomed ourselves to, in the course of the year, in the course of the weeks and months? And we stand here unshaken, untouched, inwardly unmoved!

To this message about being deeply shaken, the Second Sunday of Advent adds a new word, a message about man's *authenticity*. Someone who encounters the Ultimate, who knows about the end, must let go of every compromise. In the presence of the Ultimate the only thing that survives is what is authentic. All compromise shatters there. All cheap negotiating shatters there. All half-truths, and all double-meanings, and all masks, and all poses shatter there. The only thing that stands the test is what is authentic. It has evolved into what it was intended to become. Reality is ordered according to the authentic and healthy, to that which is true in being, and true in words, and true in deeds. Try removing from our lives—from our presence—everything that is inauthentic in being. Remove all cramps, all poses, all arrogance and hubris, and all human rebelliousness. How much of our lives disappears with these things? How much space would be freed up—and for what purpose? Really, for man, for God, and for life itself—think how much room would become free for life that is suffocating now![1] Now take from our lives all

---

[1] A reference to the word *Lebensraum*, "room for living". In Nazi ideology and propaganda, the word referred to the territorial space and environment "necessary to the autarchy of a growing nation" (Cornelia Berning, *Vom*

that is inauthentic in our speech. Take the lies away. How different relationships would be, if no one needed to figure on the other person speaking with a double meaning, or guardedly, or camouflaged—let alone deliberately lying! If a word were a word again, and a sentence were a sentence again, and a fact counted as a fact, how very different life would be!

In the Gospel for the Second Sunday of Advent, the figure of John the Baptist appears. Our Lord says of him: "What did you go out into the desert to see? A reed driven to and fro by the wind? Or what did you go out to see? A man in soft clothing? Look, those wearing soft clothing are in the palaces of kings. Or why did you go out? What did you want to see? A prophet? Yes, I say to you, and more than a prophet. This is the one of whom it is written, 'See, I send My messenger before You to prepare the way for You'" (Mt 11:7–10). This figure of John stands before us, solitary, austere, and weathered by the storms and lonelinesses of the desert and weathered by the storms and lonelinesses of the prison—but authentic.

The figure of John demonstrates two laws about authentic people and shatters two dangers to which man's authenticity generally succumbs. He shatters two situations in which an authentic man so very often suffocates and drowns. The first law and the first danger: the prophet stands before the king. And the first point: do not permit regard for private security or personal existence to make you into an inauthentic person. So very often throughout history, whenever prophet and king have encountered one another, the king is always in the superior position. What is easier, what is simpler, than to

---

"Abstammungsnachweis" zum "Zuchtwart": Vokabular des Nationalsozialismus [Berlin: Walter de Gruyter, 1964], p. 120). —Trans.

muzzle a prophet! Yet, indeed, hasn't it been—not the voices of those who went into the palaces and were welcome there—but rather the voices calling in the wilderness who filled the cosmos, who prepared the way, who directed people toward Advent, and who arranged for the proper meeting with the end and the Ultimate?

Prophet and king! The prophet must have known that the king's power and force and majesty would fall upon him and crush him if he said, "*Non licit*: That is wrong because it is inauthentic and is not in accordance with the divine order." And John said it, and he was crushed, and he was brutalized, and—for all time and eternity—he stands as the witness within history, as the witness before the face of the Lord, as authenticity itself. And he was right!

Along with that are the second law and the second danger. Futility or ineffectiveness do not dispense one from speaking the truth, declaring what is wrong, and standing up for what is right and just. How could this prophet think he could interfere in the family history and family scandals of the king, and be successful? Whoever considers success, or makes his decisions or attitudes dependent upon whether something is futile or certain of success, is already corrupt. Then authenticity no longer means his personal encounter with what is real; it is rather his personal dependence upon success, upon being heard, on popularity and applause, and on the roar of the great throngs. He is already corrupt. And woe, if the prophets are mute out of fear that their word might not be heeded.

You must let people notice that you know about the end and have grasped that one of the essential features of life is called *Advent*. And that means encounter with an Ultimate and Absolute. And that means being impressed, being forged in this loneliness with the Absolute, and therefore, whenever

it is time to give testimony, being untouched and untouch-
able when faced with compromise, half-measures, silence,
anxiety, or cowardice. May God grant that we have people,
that we have prophets, who unseal the actual meaning of
Advent to us, and who are authentic, and who offer an
authentic witness!

Homily for the Second Sunday of Advent
Preached in Munich
December 6, 1942

On the First Sunday of Advent, we talked about how, during this season of Advent, man should pray through and endure his own individual reality. We said that this saving self-knowledge should not remain purely theoretical or just words. Rather, it means decision and responsibility. A variety of responsibilities will be imposed from this time forth. We have talked about the first responsibility, about how it is our responsibility to make a disturbance in the world that is strong enough in itself to tear this chaos out of its cycle and to lead the world back to its source. Christians bear the responsibility to generate an authentic unrest within creation, through our existence, our word, and our work.

The Second Sunday in Advent points out a second responsibility today, one that weighs just as heavily on our souls. We are obliged to be concerned about the destiny of the world. Moreover, we must know that we gamble away our own individual salvation if we don't play, or, to word it better, if we don't fight, for salvation and order in the world.

Two basic ideas about this second area of responsibility are mentioned repeatedly in today's Mass. In the Introit, the Lord, the *Kyrios*, is described as God who comes *to save the nations*. This does not refer to a ghetto, but to "the nations". His will to save knows no bounds. In the Collect, we pray: Shake our hearts awake, O Lord, to prepare the way, in Your people, for Your only-begotten Son. Here the keynotes have sounded: the will to save the whole, the universal, and the will coming from a personally experienced responsibility, which demands the very beating of our hearts. The Epistle (Rom 15:4–13) says that we are of one mind, that He comes to be Lord over the nations, and that we are filled with faith, peace, joy, hope. The Gospel (Mt 11:2–10) discusses mission as necessarily stemming from personal commitment, from personal participation.

What do the old truths say about our lives today? Let us examine this from the other side. An officer serving in this war, with no connection to the Church, has written a letter in which we will recognize the second responsibility I just spoke of. I will read some passages from his letter.[1]

> From the wreckage of the medieval world view, the inevitable conclusions will be drawn. People risk setting up their material existence, dare to handle things without any sense of dependence upon a divine hand. In Nietzsche's words, "God is dead." . . . One thing is sure, if we are discussing guilt, then there is historical guilt with immense consequences, and a responsibility that neither the people of the Church, nor anyone else, can evade. Some may say, "Our dear God is dead." In any event, there can be no doubt that in the existing churches something is coming to an end.

That is the first paragraph of the letter. This God is dead, no longer plays a living role in human life. When does modern life concern itself with God? How is this or that measure, this plan, or that intention connected with the order of God? Who even asks about God? The question of the Lord God's approval has become secondary to public as well as personal life. Be honest. Ask yourself about your workdays and Sun-

---

[1] The source of this letter is not recorded. —TRANS.

days, about your plans with the youngsters. Who asks, before beginning something, "How does that fit in relationship to God's plans and commandments?" Do we not first have an idea and then ask, "Can we still combine that with God?" And then we try the cheap road of compromise. God is no longer the Lord of hearts that beat passionately for Him.

This letter continues with a question:

> How could God die? God's original message was stripped of its inherent character in three ways. First, the message was dogmatized, intercepted, and filtered. On this basis, it was not recognized as truth and was rejected. Second, the message was rationalized and left to the discretion of human reason. Sermons were institutionalized, and the pastor became an official, proclaiming the Word of God as a salaried employee. Third, the message became historicized. Jesus of Nazareth, His birth, suffering, death, and all events not comprehensible to human reason—these comprise a unique experience whose deep influence is beyond compare. Yet in the present times, a faith of this type has nothing to offer. That is how Christian talk became unworthy of belief. That is why people say that "Positive Christianity" is what is left over after all that has been stripped away.[2] The Word of God will not be heard anymore by the masses at large.

You see, a great deal in this letter is incorrect, but much is true. We need dogma and clear doctrine. We need human reason. We need history. But woe to us, if we do not have more than that! The Christian truths are treated as objects. Viewed that way, the entirety of faith is not perceived as an

---

[2] *Positive Christianity* was a term used by the "German Christians", members of a movement that attempted to combine Nazi ideology with Christianity. Parts of the Bible, including the entire Old Testament, were rejected along with any Christian teaching that was incompatible with the Nazi world view. They claimed that such "dogma" consisted of medieval innovations that should be stripped away in a "return to the source". —TRANS.

urgent presence or a real challenge to human hearts. Has anyone tried opening the catechism to experience these things, not abstractly, but as a nudge to your individual heart, to tear you away from your habitual perspective? Who has ever considered that the wonderful story of the Lord, the *Kyrios*, is not complete, but that His birth, suffering, and death should be continuing to happen anew within us and within our Church—and that then we would escape the danger of historicization, as though Christianity were merely a panacea for the old folks? Our life itself depends upon this living faith. We are no longer attending to it with heart and soul, but rather because of custom, or fear at the uncertainty of life, or scrupulosity—instead of in such a way that this universal God might, through us, touch the world and draw it home to Himself.

A third passage from the officer's experience is about awakening, and the prerequisites for an awakening.

First, in times of radical change, people experience that things have two faces. One is the foreground and one is the metaphysical background. Secondly, people become aware of the inadequacy of all things. Third, they are led to the depths of life, to the boundaries of this present world, into the midst of an environment in which the existence of a world beyond will be disputed. From this experience, there is a new piety, a chapel-less faith[3] that God who has been declared "dead" is not dead—that He is daily influencing the world—that our existence is ordered not only by the cosmic component, but each individual is guided by a personal spiritual source. Such people can be recognized by their commitment to teamwork and by their leadership, obedience, and

---

[3] "Chapel-less faith" is a term coined by Rainer Maria Rilke in his poem "Wunderweiße Nächte" (R. M. Rilke, *Traumgekrönte—Neue Gedichte* [Leipzig: Friesenhahn Verlag, 1897], p. 31). —TRANS.

responsibility. They have the courage to see the world as it is, and when something goes wrong, to look for the fault within themselves. They are contradictory people, hard as diamonds and yet gentle and sensitive.

That, indeed, is what a Christian should be like, a person of quiet readiness and interior vigor. We should live deeply centered in the Holy Spirit. Now you have the second responsibility: that we should burn with a desire to save the peoples and not focus on our own little egos. Where there is talk about joy, peace, and overflowing hope, there you will find vital personalities who give the lie to all that outcry about God being dead. On the one hand, Christian life is much simpler, but on the other hand, it is much more difficult, just because a great life must be taken seriously. The Christian must always view things from the great perspective of God and live accordingly.

This second responsibility is the question about each individual's own personal vitality and whether this vitality concentrates itself into the resolution to do everything possible to save people and to establish God's order and God's Kingdom. Our hearts must be keenly alert for opportunities in our own little corners of daily life. May we stand in this world, not as people in hiding, but as those who help prepare the way of the only-begotten Son of God.

Meditation for the Second Sunday of Advent
Written in Tegel Prison, Berlin
December 1944

"Surge et sta in excelso—Arise and stand on high" (Bar 5:5). Value or lack of value, depth or lack of depth in human life depends greatly upon life remaining sculptured, knowing and affirming all of its dimensions, and not rendering itself innocuous by flattening out or encapsulating itself into insignificance. Foreshortening and falsification of perspectives with loss of the full dimensions come under the heading of general Occidental development and individual personal development. We are the result. This has to do with risks that always accompany human idiosyncrasy, but in our generation these have increased and become more widespread.

The great historical and personal hours of grace will always mean some form of awakening and return to a true order of reality. This is also the meaning of Advent: not only promise, but rather conversion and transformation. Plato would say, "Orientation to a capability for truth". John the Baptist put it more simply, "Repent" (Mt 3:2). The prayers and messages of Advent push man out beyond every surface and bring him to a consciousness of the full sculptural dimensions and drama of his situation.

Therefore, the First Sunday had the recurring theme of violent shaking. Revelation of man's vulnerable situation (see the Gospel and second half of the Collect). Movement toward God, out of that self-certain autarchy. Life's central priority is within this movement (Introit, Epistle, Gradual, Offertory, etc.). Calling upon the divine freedom to come and meet the helpless motion of our powerlessness (Collect from First Sunday: "Excita potentiam tuam . . . [Awaken Your power . . .]").

The Second Sunday directs these thoughts further and concretizes them through personal decision. The message contains three clear statements.

The first statement:

—God's promise to continue this movement toward man. God is always the One who is coming, but not just some day in the future; He is right now, and always, in the process of coming (Introit, Epistle, Gospel, Secret).

—God's promise that He comes as the God who wants to heal and save (Introit and Gospel, first half).

—The challenge to mankind to take this God seriously, "ut abundetis in spe . . . [that you may overflow with hope . . .]" (Rom 15:13). A person filled with confidence in God will profit from this time and stand up to the test.

The second statement:

—This has nothing to do with trivializing or flattening life out, as if there were some bourgeois existence connected with the divine. God's blessing takes neither the pleasure of freedom away from us, nor its burden. The encounter with this God who wants to save is not arranged according to our discretion, nor in the way or the place we might choose.

—Thus, in the midst of this message for the Second Sunday of Advent, we read the Word of the Lord: "And blessed is he who does not take offense at Me" (Mt 11:6). That means that God is on the way, but He has His own style, His own ways of coming. It means that anyone who makes his salvation dependent upon his own personal taste is a lost man.

—Furthermore, this means that the concrete place to find this healing movement is the encounter with Christ. The way of salvation for the world is the way of the Savior. There is no other. One must see this and say it clearly, not water it down.

The third statement gives this Sunday its theme: *decision for salvation in Christ.*

—As a decision for eternal life (Postcommunion). This "amare cælestia [love of heavenly things]"[1] is a difficult and important matter.

—As a decision for freedom from petty entanglements and viewpoints: "Surge et sta in excelso [Rise up and stand on high]" (Communion Prayer). The lofty standpoint determines the field of vision a life will have and gives the air that a soul breathes.

—As a decision for character and attitude (Gospel: the austere figure of John the Baptist, Mt 11:2–10).

—As a decision for Christian mission: individual salvation comes only through this commitment to the Christianization of life, through the personal bond with the figure and mission of Christ Himself (Gospel, Collect).

—As a decision that is a grace, activated within us by the Lord: as in the Collect: "Excita corda nostra . . . [Awaken

---

[1] From the Closing Prayer of the Second Sunday of Advent: *amare cælestia.*

our hearts . . .]", which is the counterpart to last Sunday's "Excita potentiam tuam [Awaken Your power]." May God break open the narrowness that confines us within ourselves, and make us capable of Him, and capable of His mission.[2]

So this Sunday too, we need to fold our hands again, and bend our knees and bow our egos in adoration before God, so that His salvation can be effective in us and make us capable of being called and touched by Him. All of modern arrogance breaks down here, but at the same time, all of our helplessness and loneliness—in which we often almost freeze to death[3]—will be opened up and filled with divine warmth and healed by divine consecration.

---

[2] In earlier writings, Fr. Delp stated that modern man is "no longer capable of God". The reference is to *capax dei*: "The mind is the image of God, in that it is capable of God and can be partaker of Him" (St. Augustine, *De Trinitate*, 14, 8:11). See also "Meditation for the Christmas Vigil, 1944". —TRANS.

[3] Compare "Figures of Advent", *The Blessed Mother*: "What use to us is this shivering from cold and hardship, in which the world is freezing to death the more it loses and deadens itself deep down inside, if we do not at the same time experience that grace which is mightier than the danger and the lostness?" —TRANS.

Advent Holy Hour

God does not need great pathos or great works,
but He needs greatness of hearts.
He cannot calculate with zeroes.

— Alfred Delp, S.J.
  Advent Holy Hour, 1942

Meditation for an Advent Holy Hour
Munich
December 1942

We want to recall briefly the reason and intention of our Holy Hour. These fateful days have hit us all hard, and we feel it. We want something more than this suffering and worry and visible distress we have been going through. God the Lord is present in everything that happens, and we want to find the answer to all this that He wants from us. We want to arrive at that composure and harmony of heart that God surely wants to accomplish in us and that we owe to Him. Without it, He will not avert the distress of this world from us.

We do not want to gather together here only to beg. We want to step into the ranks of the great intercessors, to approach the question that is God's challenge to us. Through His Spirit, we must increase the world's proper order and responsibility, its proper composure, so that it is in harmony with God, so that the intrinsic lack of peace, from which all suffering and distress comes, will end! This intrinsic lack of peace within the world is because man's dispositions are no longer in conformity with God's freedom or the questions He daily poses to us.[1]

---

[1] God's freedom was another favorite term in Fr. Delp's preaching. A concise definition: "Divine freedom is positively to be defined as *libertas contradictionis*, that is, freedom to act or not to act (for example, to create the world), and as *libertas specificationis*, that is, freedom to choose between various good

79

If we as victims succeed in communicating this through silent example and enlightening word, and if we make it the rule and order of our days, it will show that we have been authentic worshippers. We will have come before God in truth and freedom, as authentic *pacifici* [peacemakers].

Let us not just go begging during this Holy Hour and think only of our own concerns. Instead, let us come as representatives for all the lost people, as intercessors and representatives for a troubled, beaten, and spiritually helpless mankind. You can see for yourselves how, after a couple of days of quiet, so many of us have already begun to forget again. We act as if nothing had happened. Some kind of interior agitation and awakening has not yet reached many of us, even with the terror we have just gone through.

Let us fill this hour of prayer with the old readiness that comes from a new perspective. Let us simply fill it with the religious meaning of the day we are celebrating. We are making this hour of pilgrimage today in Advent on the day of the Sacred Heart of Jesus,[2] and we approach the motherly Queen of Heaven and Earth.

First, it is a Holy Hour in Advent. Advent is really the great freedom of God. May man recognize this freedom of God in God's free decision to come to mankind—as well as the freedom of God in His choice of the ways and means in which He wants to meet us. God can stand before mankind in a burning thorn bush or in the miracle of His Son, in times and days of distress and in times of mercy, in order to lift man beyond himself so he can meet God in freedom. God is not

---

or indifferent actions (for example, to create this or that world)" (Ludwig Ott, *Fundamentals of Catholic Dogma*, trans. P. Lynch [Cork: Mercier Press, 1955], p. 47). —TRANS.

[2] The references to the Sacred Heart indicate that this was a First Friday Holy Hour, which would have been December 4, 1942. —TRANS.

bound to a particular way of coming to us. He can be more motherly than a mother, or He can stand as the God of all destinies, writing the word of the Lordship of God hard and ineradicably upon human consciousness, because we did not understand it in those days when all was going well for us.

Perhaps we sense something of the sovereignty of God again and know that everything is in His hands. Perhaps we sense it again as the world falls into horror, which somehow thoroughly mocks all our predictions and opinions and protective measures. Advent means remembering the freedom of God and then abandoning ourselves to the divine unpredictability.

The freedom of God is at the same time, however, the grace of God, the God who is coming to us. And our hearts must be alert and ready to feel the Lord God, who seeks our souls and whose world, basically, is in its proper order only when our hearts and His heart beat together in one rhythm. God's deepest intention is to keep pursuing man until mankind yields and man believes in the grace and consecration of life again. So Advent means a heart that is awake and ready, which does not let itself become encrusted, or bitter and deadened through hard blows, but stays awake and aware of the free coming of the Lord God. That is why this free God must be met by a free person, by someone who is free beyond hardship, beyond desires, beyond worry: someone who may well suffer from these things, but without going under.

It ultimately has to do with this intrinsic freedom that transcends the material, transcends the human level: that there be people again who bow down before the Lord in reverence and true adoration, that there be people again with the proper perspective on life. That is the message of this day today: that there needs to be people again who live life in its proper form. Our lifestyle is not simply left to our discretion.

No, it is really a consequence of the fact that God is the Lord and that we are the creatures.

Secondly, there is a form to our existence. The *Cor Jesu* [the Sacred Heart of Jesus], the ardent heart of God, stands here before us proclaiming two messages. The first message is that there is no merely human life anymore. Man is real only as a divine-human type. Where this mysterious covenant has not occurred, there is not just a lack of some kind of ornament or extra. What is lacking is the peg that supports the whole, and the inner strength that holds everything together. If man does not come out beyond himself into this intimacy with God, letting the divinely merciful reality flow in, then he is "too modest" and less than himself. He drops out of the only valid form of life and no longer has the strength to be human as he should be—as he must be—in order to breathe freely. Divine-human order is the only order of our lives.

Cor Jesu stands before mankind with the wounds He bears in the center of His heart. A deeply essential feature of our life is visible here. Even from the natural perspective, the idea of sacrifice belongs to the structure of life. It belongs even more to the structure of Christian life. If you are not capable of standing before the community and somehow taking their deepest needs upon yourself—coming before the Lord God and taking on the guilt, taking on the punishment—without this capability, then you still lack a great deal before you can justly bear the name and call yourself Christian, and let yourself appear in the presence of God. God does not need great pathos or great works, but He needs greatness of hearts. He cannot calculate with zeroes. When man is confronted with who he is, He wants him to accept himself entirely, to commit himself totally, and to contribute all he can.

Third, the basic word of the Mother of the Lord needs to be repeated, that Yes that knows all destiny and takes on the burden of every destiny. We can reflect for a moment how it might have been if Mary had not received the message of God with this readiness and freedom to give herself to God. What if Mary had said No? Perhaps God's plan would have been postponed. God might have taken a different route. Yet what would have happened to the human being, to Mary? Her life would have shattered. Spiritually it would have been a failure, a negated life that had denied its true fulfillment. This is not just an incidental thought.

We have become accustomed to the idea that what God asks of us, the great basic teachings of our lives, and the great responses required by God are somehow accessories—as if we can take them or leave them—as if they are just trinkets for those who choose to accept them. We have very often forgotten that the God of freedom—the God of grace and divine humanity—is a God who challenges us. God wants to be taken seriously, wants to be all, not just an accessory. He does not just leave it to chance whether we say Yes or No. A time comes where our refusal is refusing the fulfillment of our lives, because we have not taken God into account and have not dealt with the Lord God in discernment. He is a God who challenges. What transformed the person, Mary, into the motherly Queen of Heaven and Earth is that she recognized God as a God of challenge. She experienced what it means to be torn away from all normal destinies and, thereby, to be caught up in new possibilities. She stands as a healing and helping source of strength, right in the middle of what no one can know beforehand. Now for us, it is about doing these two things right: saying Yes, and obtaining new possibilities of helping strength for others.

Week III

Are you a person
whose concerns are with God?
Are you a person of whom it can be said
that your heart and your mind are filled
with a peace that surpasses all comprehension?
Oh, that we could be such people again,
intrinsically filled to the brim—
not only with the knowledge,
but with the personal, prayed-in,
and wrestled-in reality and abundance
of our Lord God!

— Alfred Delp, S.J.
  Third Sunday of Advent, 1944

Liturgy for the Third Sunday of Advent

Introit: Philippians 4:4–6, Psalm 85(84):2

Gaudete in Domino semper: iterum dico, gaudete. Modestia vestra nota sit omnibus hominibus: Dominus enim prope est. Nihil solliciti sitis: sed in omni oratione petitiones vestræ innotescant apud Deum. Benedixisti, Domine, terram tuam: avertisti captivitatem Jacob. Gloria Patri, et Filio, et Spiritui Sancto. Sicut erat in principio, et nunc, et semper, et in sæcula sæculorum. Amen.

Rejoice in the Lord always. Once again, I say: rejoice. Let all people experience your modesty. The Lord is near. Do not worry about anything, but continue to make your needs known to God in heartfelt prayer. Lord, You have blessed Your land and averted Jacob's captivity. Glory be to the Father, and to the Son, and to the Holy Spirit. As it was in the beginning, is now, and ever shall be, world without end. Amen.

Collect:

Aurem tuam, quæsumus, Domine, precibus nostris accomoda: et mentis nostræ tenebras, gratia tuæ visitationis illustra: Qui vivis et regnas cum Deo Patre in unitate Spiritus Sancti, Deus, per omnia sæcula sæculorum. Amen.

Give ear to our prayer, we beseech You, O Lord, and make bright the darkness of our minds through the grace of Your coming: You who live and reign with God the Father in the unity of the Holy Spirit, God, for ever and ever. Amen.

Epistle: Philippians 4:4–7

Fratres: Gaudete in Domino semper: iterum dico, gaudete. Modestia vestra nota sit omnibus hominibus: Dominus prope est. Nihil solliciti sitis: sed in omni oratione et obsecratione, cum gratiarum actione, petitiones vestræ innotescant apud Deum. Et pax Dei, quæ exsuperat omnem sensum, custodiat corda vestra et intelligentias vestras, in Christo Jesu Domino nostro.

Brethren: Rejoice in the Lord always. Once again, I say: rejoice. Let all people experience your goodness and modesty. The Lord is near. Do not worry about anything, but in everything, make your petitions known to God in heartfelt prayer and supplication, with thanksgiving. And the peace of God that passes all understanding preserve your hearts and thoughts, in Christ Jesus our Lord.

Gradual: Psalm 80(79):2–3

Qui sedes, Domine, super Cherubim, excita potentiam tuam, et veni. V. Qui regis Israël, intende: qui deducis, velut ovem, Joseph.

Lord, You who are enthroned above the cherubim, awaken Your power and come.
V. Attend, you leaders of Israel, you who lead Joseph like a sheep.

Alleluia: Psalm 80(79):2

*Alleluia, alleluia.
V. Excita, Domine, potentiam tuam, et veni, ut salvos facias nos. Alleluia.*

Alleluia, alleluia.

V. Awaken Your power, O Lord, and come to redeem us.
Alleluia.

Gospel: John 1:19–28

*In illo tempore: Miserunt Judæi ab Jerosolymis sacerdotes et levitas ad
Joannem, ut interrogarent eum: Tu quis es? Et confessus est, et non
negavit: et confessus est: Quia non sum ego Christus. Et inter-
rogaverunt eum: Quid ergo? Elias es tu? Et dixit: Non sum.
Propheta es tu? Et respondit: Non. Dixerunt ergo ei: Quis es, ut
responsum demus his, qui miserunt nos? Quid dicis de teipso? Ait:
Ego vox clamantis in deserto: Dirigite viam Domini, sicut dixit
Isaias propheta. Et qui missi fuerant, erant ex pharisæis. Et
interrogaverunt eum, et dixerunt ei: Quid ergo baptizas, si tu non es
Christus, neque Elias, neque propheta? Respondit eis Joannes, dicens:
Ego baptizo in aqua: medius autem vestrum stetit, quem vos nescitis.
Ipse est, qui post me venturus est, qui ante me factus est: cujus
ego non sum dignus, ut solvam ejus corrigiam calceamenti. Hæc in
Bethania facta sunt trans Jordanem, ubi erat Joannes baptizans.*

At that time, the Jews sent priests and Levites from Jerusalem
to John to ask him, "Who are you?" Then he confessed and
did not deny, and he confessed, "I am not the Christ." And
they asked him, "Who are you then? Are you Elijah?" And
he said, "No, I am not." "Are you the prophet?" He answered, "No." Then they said to him, "Who are you that we
may give an answer to those who sent us. What do you have
to say for yourself?" He said, "I am the voice crying in the
wilderness. 'Make straight the way of the Lord,' as the
prophet Isaiah said." And they who had been sent were
Pharisees. And they questioned him, asking, "Why do you
baptize if you are not Christ, or Elijah, or the prophet?" John

answered them, saying, "I baptize with water, but in your midst stands One whom you do not know. It is He who will come after me, who preceded me, whose sandal I am not worthy to untie." This took place in Bethany, beyond the Jordan, where John was baptizing.

Offertory: Psalm 85(84):2

Benedixisti, Domine, terram tuam: avertisti captivitatem Jacob: remisisti iniquitatem plebis tuæ.

Lord, You have blessed Your land and averted Jacob's captivity. You have forgiven the iniquity of Your people.

Secret:

Devotionis nostræ tibi, quæsumus, Domine, hostia jugiter immoletur: quæ et sacri peragat institua mysterii, et salutare tuum in nobis mirabiliter operetur. Per Dominum nostrum Jesum Christum, Filium tuum, qui tecum vivit et regnat in unitate Spiritus Sancti, Deus, per omnia sæcula sæculorum. Amen.

We beseech You, O Lord, that this sacrifice of our devotion may be offered continually to You, to effect Your purposes in these holy mysteries and to work in us the wonders of Your salvation. Through our Lord Jesus Christ, Your Son, who lives and reigns with You in the unity of the Holy Spirit, God, for ever and ever. Amen.

Communion: Isaiah 35:4

Dicite: pusillanimes, confortamini et nolite timere: ecce Deus noster veniet et salvabit nos.

Announce: "You faint-hearted ones, be comforted and do not be afraid, for behold, our God will come and save us."

Postcommunion:

Imploramus Domine, clementiam tuam: ut hæc divina subsidia, a vitiis expiatos, ad festa ventura nos præparent. Per Dominum nostrum Jesum Christum, Filium tuum, qui tecum vivit et regnat in unitate Spiritus Sancti, Deus, per omnia sæcula sæculorum. Amen.

We implore Your clemency, O Lord. May these divine means cleanse us from our sins and prepare us for this coming feast. Through our Lord Jesus Christ, Your Son, who lives and reigns with You in the unity of the Holy Spirit, God, for ever and ever. Amen.

Homily for the Third Sunday of Advent
Preached in Munich
December 14, 1941

"And they asked him, 'Who are you?'" (Jn 1:19). Over the previous Sundays, we apprehended and understood Advent as the encounter of man with, the journey of man toward, the Ultimate, toward the Absolute, toward the Lord God. Standing in the presence of the Last Things, in the presence of the Ultimate, resulted in—and results in—a peculiar knowledge of ourselves. From this holy place of encounter we have perceived two Advent messages.

Here is the first message: Man facing the Ultimate must be someone in a state of being shaken, with an alert, awakened heart that does not freeze up, does not become weary, or cramped, or deadened, but sees things as they are. Someone facing the Ultimate will not be apathetic, not just accept everything simply because it is, and because it does not change, and because it goes on and on, and because it is happening everywhere.

And that brings us to the second message, the message of authenticity, which says: In the presence of God, the Absolute Ultimate, nothing counts but that which is real. Man can pass the test of the last days only without pathos, without cramps, without lies, without masks. This requires an honesty of being that has measured itself against the Ultimate, an honesty of being that, in the presence of the Ultimate, passes the test.

Moreover, out of this encounter with the Last Things and the Ultimate, a third Advent message comes to us today. The austere figure of John the Baptist stands before us again, toughened by the thousand lonelinesses of the desert, consecrated and spiritually molded by the thousand other lonelinesses of his encounters with the Lord God: his consecration, his mission, his vocation. And the people go to John and ask, "Who are you?" That is the third message of Advent, and it means *confession*.[1] Direct questions and direct answers. John stands there, this strange person, a halo, an air of the supernatural about him, a power for touching hearts. The people start moving; the crowd gathers around him. They stand there and ask a question. Basically, this is the most seductive question ever posed to those who have been given power over the hearts of the people. "Are you the Messiah? Are you the prophet? Are you the Holy One of the last days?" Oh, that is the temptation which comes over anyone who is any kind of public figure whom the people follow! That is the temptation. This question, or this challenge, or this deceit: "Are you the Messiah? Are you the Christ? Are you the man of salvation? Are you the man of the Last Judgment? Are you he who is to come?"

How often history's leaders, who were entrusted with a great mandate for the organization and order of the world, have been defeated by this seduction! Instead of salvation they brought disaster, because they were not honest enough to confess to themselves and to others: "No." The cornerstone of every such confession is modesty, and the knowledge of limits and of areas of responsibility. It is the knowledge that, precisely in connection to the Last Things,

---

[1] The German word *Bekenntnis* and the English "confession" encompass a similar range of meanings. The sense intended here is that of public declaration and affirmation of belief in something. —TRANS.

every overstepping of boundaries, every boundary violation and every usurping of power leads the whole thing to disaster. Look at how these great leaders were shattered and how their work was shattered: Alexander, Caesar Augustus, Napoleon, and a hundred others from the realms of intellect and the arts. It came when they were not content with the laurel wreath of greatness, but wanted to take the diadem of the Messiah, the proclamation of salvation, the ultimate jurisdiction for themselves as well. John the Baptist is asked, "Who are you?" and he answers, "I am not the Christ." That is the one side of the message about confession, that one must know and must loudly proclaim the truth. From this standpoint, for the sake of salvation, for the sake of the whole, one must contradict false claims when they are set forth or intimated, and false promotions when they are offered. That is the one side.

The other side, which sets it apart from the first and which applies to each one of us, is the question, directed personally to each one, "Who are you?" This is asked clearly and explicitly. One day, when we stand in the presence of the Absolute, this question will cut through our existence like a lightning bolt and manifest what is real and what was masquerade. If we are honest, even now, it sometimes must shudder through our being that the question, "Who are you?" will be posed to us. This lightning bolt examination will not only pose the question from without, through those who will ask us and who do ask us every hour. It will not only address our work, our word, and our allegiance. It will address our very selves. "Who are you?"

Confession has absolutely never meant blind allegiance to a program, protocol, or proclamation. Mankind has been duped by such formulated paragraphs, such numbered, legal declarations, since time immemorial. Confession is threefold.

It is primarily a matter of being. It is, beyond all words and beyond all pathos, a matter of what is real. In the Epistle today, we read: "Worry about nothing." Then your prayer and pleading, offered with thanksgiving, will be made known to God. And may the peace of God, which surpasses all comprehension, keep your hearts and your thoughts in Christ Jesus, our Lord.

When the Christian is asked, or asks himself, "Who are you?" this is primarily a questioning of his reality: Are you a person whose concerns are with God? Are you a person of whom it can be said that your heart and your mind are filled with a peace that surpasses all comprehension? Oh, that we could be such people again, intrinsically filled to the brim— not only with the knowledge, but with the personal, prayed-in and wrestled-in reality and abundance of our Lord God! That is the first thing confession means, which sets it apart from false presumption: being present, authentically standing up and standing for something real. Perhaps there has been too much talk about Christians and about Christian life by people who, one notices, are not speaking from experience. They do not personally know the abundance that simply flows forth from those who are fulfilled, who know no other and seek no other than what is truly real. The world, and life, and space are subject to reality, not just to words or protest or any kind of intrigue. Therefore, confession means confessing to our very being, and its capability of allegiance and capability of bearing responsibility.

Confession also means confessing to an assignment. "*Who are you?*" The austere figure of John the Baptist stands there and says: "*I am the voice crying in the wilderness.*" Confession means proclaiming, praising, and really spreading the word. The voice is that of a caller, a seeker, someone really driven from within and touched by the Lord God's restlessness:

Someone who goes through this wilderness among mankind
again and again as the Seeker, and as the Caller. You can sense
that this is more than the call of a man, or a power, or a
greatness, or a thirst for dominance, or a violent force. This is
the Calling-God, who calls out in the midst of the wilderness
through voices of men. He has filled them, and their very
being documents that such perfected people are among us,
sent by God.

All of this, the capability of confessing through one's very
existence, as well as through calling and through giving testimony, can emerge only from the third meaning of confession. It means confessing allegiance to a belief, to a real faith.
John said, "I baptize with water, but in your midst stands One
whom you do not know" (Jn 1:26). Oh, that once again
people could readily perceive our enthrallment, our true,
ultimate allegiance to this One, to this Christ, in whose
Advent we stand! That will be the question, and it will be the
decisive question. Will we succeed once more in loving this
Christ—in loving Him as personally as only a man, a woman,
a mature person can love—so that we are touched and moved
and swept away by an ultimate reality? *In your midst stands One
whom you do not know.* He is, however, in our words and in the
beating of our hearts and the hammering of our pulses and in
everything. What you do not comprehend, and yet what
should be so real and merciful, is that He is standing there,
through it all, in your midst. That should be our confession.
It is not a protest, not a proclamation, but our very being,
consecrated by the Lord God, testifying for itself and for the
Lord God, for Christ, who is our mystery, but who is also our
strength and our certainty, and whose Advent alone is the
one and only salvation of the world.

Homily for the Third Sunday of Advent Preached in Munich December 13, 1942

Today, for the third time, we want to speak about this holy season. It is not only that Advent is one of the primeval tides of the human soul, in which we become conscious of reaching out to grasp eternal things; it is not only a dawning of the eternal connections, that man is a wayfarer, is under way, and sometimes wounds himself trying to grasp the eternal. Twice we have said that the meaning must condense itself into responsibility; the responsibility must become a tremendous personal responsibility that is oriented solely to the measure of God and knows only the message of God, soaked into an utterly surrendered heart. It is a responsibility that is laid upon our hearts and our minds. We must take this seriously, for ourselves and for our people.

Three statements stand out today in the Mass texts. The first message is: "Lord, make bright the darkness of our minds" (Collect). This means we should recognize that there are things that will not be seen. There are decisive hours in history, when what is essential will not be seen and people will get lost following a lesser value. This darkness, this deluded mind, is expressed in a song of darkness that has appeared on the German Christmas market this season:

The world no longer is the same
Since that Galilean came.
His deeply shaking call rang out:
"The world is poor",
And as He died they heard Him shout:
"It is finished",
While clinking glasses briskly ring:
"The beauty of the world—a lovely thing!"
The Christ, however, strictly told
That God forbade that toast of old.
Shattered idols from their places torn.
How changed the heartbeats seem to mourn,
Since that day He spoke the word:
"The world is sinful." [1]

Do we not have reason to sink to our knees and ask God to open our eyes and show us the core meaning of the whole?

A second word from the Gospel is: "And they went out to ask John: 'Who are you?' 'I am the voice calling in the wilderness'", and so on (Jn 1:23). You have known this passage for a long time, but we do not want to overlook this one reference, that of moderation. Here is a word to John that offers the man a great opportunity to stand on the summit, at least for an hour. The ability to hold to moderation is a lesson for us and for our times. A book, *The Endless Reformation*,[2] has appeared. It claims that the German people are called to knock down all boundaries, never to stop. That is our mission, never to attend or listen reverently, but rather to hammer high-handedly on the gates of divinity, overturning

---

[1] The source of this poem is not recorded. —TRANS.
[2] Friedrich Parpert, *Die endlose Reformation* (Munich: Reinhardt Verlag, 1939).

everything. A song of immoderation. This book discusses only the trinity of struggle, movement, and progress. Yet here, in the Gospel, is the news of moderation, the definitive message of modesty for our times.

Then we read this wonderful epistle: "Brethren, rejoice in the Lord . . . and the peace of God that passes all understanding preserve your hearts and thoughts in Christ Jesus, our Lord" (Phil 4:4–7). Are these not images of the promise, and longing, and great questions of Advent? Are they not images of what should be fulfilled when the veils fall, when the Lord reigns over the land? Do we not seek a life in which joy would have a place once again? I refer to that joy Thomas Aquinas called "A well-being of the spirit in response to what exists",[3] that is, joy in response to those things granted by God. How we cry out for a sign that we really walk in the light, and that we will not be handed over on Judgment Day! How we long to see things become stable and reliable! Look at this other theme in the Epistle: "Let all people experience your goodness, for the Lord is near!" How the world would be transformed if we could feel that each person we met were well-meaning! People, how lovely life would be again! "Do not worry about anything." Oh, if the overwhelming over-load of worry were banned—the worry about daily bread, about necessary freedom of movement, about those dear people who continually face danger and destruction—if all this could be seen in its proper perspective!

"And the peace of God . . ." Oh, if the world would only hear these words and morally wake up! When will people finally cease destroying each other?

Many regard these images to be hallucinations and delusions. Listen to the sorrowful song of our times:

---

[3] Compare Thomas Aquinas, *Summa theologica*, Ia IIae, q. 31, a. 1.

> You are so lonely, man.
> The world so great is still and numb,
> A ghost town waiting for ghosts to come . . .

That is a song of despair, a song of nothingness. Yet here is our message: "*Rejoice!*" and from this recognition comes the third responsibility for the true awakening of the spirits, minds, and hearts of our people. The principal clause says: "for the Lord is near". The prerequisite is that our minds be "undarkened" so the Lord will bless His land once again. That is why this great responsibility is laid upon us. Do you know what's going on? It is about this one thing. Will the image of the Lord's blessing shining through this people be fulfilled once again, or will the curse of despair smother us? Woe to those who just think to themselves, "I am righteous, because I still believe and I still pray. . .", while a people, a generation, an entire continent is running off into the night. We have to bear this responsibility. We will have no Christmas if we neglect it, if we do not call out, "Look, the Lord is waiting and must be near!" so that the German heart will wake up and see the true values, in true proportion, and find the way back to the Lord, the *Kyrios*.

Meditation for the Third Sunday of Advent
Written in Tegel Prison, Berlin
December 1944

The Conditions for True Joy

Well now, what is joy, true joy? The philosophers say it is satisfaction and emotional uplift in response to the goods at one's disposal. That may be true of some phenomena of joy, but it is not joy itself. Otherwise, how could I attain to true joy in these times and in this situation?

Is there any point in bothering about joy? Is joy not among those luxury items of life that have no place in the meager private area tolerated in wartime conversations? Certainly it has no place in a prison cell where someone is pacing back and forth, his hands in irons, his heart swelled by all the winds of longing, his head filled with worries and questions.

Someone must experience such a situation, must have it happen time and again, that suddenly the heart no longer can grasp the abundance of inflowing life and happiness, that suddenly, and without knowing why or how, the flags are in place once again over existence, and promises are valid again. One time or another, it might be the self-defense mechanism of existence fighting against crushing abuse and violation—but not every time. It was so often a presentiment of good news on the way—such things do happen in our Monastery of the Hard Life. And often, soon afterward, resourceful love found a way to us with a gift of kindness at a time when this was not customary.[1]

However, that was not all. There have been, and continue to be, times where one is comforted and spiritually uplifted: times where one sees the facts of the case exactly as real and hopeless as ever and yet is not grieved by it, but truly manages to turn the whole thing over to the Lord.

Now, that is the decisive word. Joy in human life has to do with God. Creatures can bring us joy in various forms and can provide an occasion for joy and rejoicing, but the actual success of this depends upon whether we are still capable of joy and familiar with it. And that, again, is conditional upon our personal relationship to the Lord God.

Only in God is man fully capable of life. Without Him, over time, we become sick. This sickness attacks our joy and our capability for joy. That is why man, when he still had time, made so much noise about joy. In the end, even that was no longer permitted. The prison-world took him over so completely that even joy was valued and presented only as a means to employ for a new end.

In order to be capable of true life, man must live according to a specific order and relationship to God. The capability of true joy and of living joyfully is itself dependent upon specific conditions of human life, upon particular attitudes regarding God. Where life does not perceive itself as taking

[1] This comparison of prison life to a cloistered, penitential religious order also appears in Fr. Delp's prison letters. During the night of August 14, in agony and despair after weeks of isolation and torture, he prayed for release through death or for an opportunity to escape. His prayer was answered, not with the release he longed for, but with a powerful experience of spiritual consolation and peace. The next day, unexpectedly, "resourceful love" found a way to him. A "gift of kindness" from Marianne Hapig and Marianne Pünder was the first of many packets of food, clean laundry, and other gifts (ADGS, 4:29, 292). —TRANS.

place in community with God, it will be gray and gloomy and drab and calculating.

How should we live so that we are capable—or can become capable—of true joy? This question should occupy us more today than it has in the past. Man should take joy as seriously as he takes himself. And he should believe in himself, believe in his heart and in his Lord God, even through darkness and distress—that he is created for joy. This really means that we are created for a fulfilled life that knows its meaning and is certain of its capabilities. Such a life knows it is on the right path to perfection and allied with the angels and powers of God. We are created for a life that knows itself to be blessed, sent, and touched at its deepest center by God Himself.

How should man live so that this happiness begins to grow in his heart, giving his eyes and face a brilliant shine and his hands a satisfying ability and success?

Five conditions for true joy and the capability of joy are named in today's Gaudete Sunday liturgy. The meditative reflection upon these conditions for true joy is, at once, both a personal examination of conscience and a historical consideration of the development of joylessness in modern life. How could the substitute for joy spread itself so broadly that people now call "joy" what they never would have looked at or touched when they were healthy human beings? Perhaps we can regain a sense of what was within the saints, those great people who were capable of joy and whose eyes seemed made for the discovery of sources of joy everywhere. Saint Francis' "Canticle to the Sun" is not mere lyrical rambling. It expresses the great inner freedom that enabled him to observe the intrinsic value and discover the fulfilling assignment within all things.

The conditions for true joy have nothing to do with

conditions of our exterior life, but consist of man's interior frame of mind and competence, which make it possible now and again for him to sense, even in adverse external circumstances, what life is basically about.

I.

Today, with Saint Paul, the liturgy names the first prerequisite for making true joy possible: "In Domino [In the Lord]. Gaudete in Domino [Rejoice in the Lord]. Dominus prope est [The Lord is near]" (Phil 4:4–5).

Holiness and happiness intrinsically belong together. To the intellectual and challenging perspective of one who seeks to understand the whole, both the question of religiousness, as well as the question of joyous fulfillment versus joyless emptiness and desert wilderness, present themselves in an inseparable manner—whether applied to an era, a culture, or a personal life.

Moreover, they present themselves in a double sense. The first sense is that of the First Commandment. Life is ruled by eternal lordship and eternal order. It has to do with eternal values and attitudes. "Dominus prope est [The Lord is near]" must then mean that people have let this nearness sink into their consciousness, not merely into their memories, or into the repertoire of truths of which preachers regularly remind them. Then man can maintain the necessary tension, which is the only way a moral-eternal being can live. Then the abundance of reality is not a jumble of variables to which man attains, according to the various values he assigns to them; instead, it follows a hierarchically established order. Then man escapes the greedy imposition of a value that tries to own him, or at least he finds a fixed standpoint from which he can afford defense and resistance.

At the same time, however, the liturgy names the great joy-killers to which the godless life has abandoned itself. If man excludes himself from the temporal-eternal tension, he will be strangled by the senselessness that permeates everything and that forces itself upon him as the result of his life. Then he will fall into the confusion of an unenlightened existence, into whose twilight no illuminating sun can break through to him. He will find himself distracted by the multiplicity and the opposition of the various values to one another, if no divine order prioritizes his tastes, works, and affections. In the end, he will succumb to the barbarism of the most popular values and the most trivial material goods of the time. He will be possessed and hunted and driven, no longer a free man and no longer master. Through all of this, he is not merely offered certain basic experiences of existence that everyone must pass through, but is instead delivered over to them. He has fallen into the experience of limitation. He experiences himself, and the world, and all things as limitations, even though the colorful wings of his mind, of his yearnings, press beyond all limits. Left to his own devices, he cannot rise above these limitations. He falls prey to the impression that the world is futile and, what is worse, that human life is futile. At this point, he is in danger of remaining stuck in that experience of melancholy into which fate sends him again and again, because he no longer hears the intrinsic message of circumstances and the intrinsic song of events. The world readily becomes a place without comfort, to which it is hardly worthwhile to become accustomed, although he does not know any way out. Alternatively, all these experiences, which repeatedly offer opportunities for a view of the whole, can be rashly passed over and a cheap "Carpe diem! [Seize the day!]" raised as a colorful banner. The great deception begins, the time of noise and crowds, organized feeding-frenzies, and massive festivities. Until suddenly the earth quakes and the sub-terranean thunder—which one wanted to drown out with screaming, because one failed to understand it—breaks forth fully and mightily and fills the day with its call to judgment.

That is the path—of a people, of a generation, of an indi-vidual—into the wasteland and void of a life without joy. Moreover, if people and things are permitted to remain in this condition, it will only get worse. An aversion to one another has seized hold of creation. The harmonic song of the spheres dissipates in an orgy of gore and of willful annihi-lation that creatures are beginning to perpetrate against all creation.

Only one thing will help, and that is to hear the call of John the Baptist. The great conversion will consecrate and transform the wilderness for mankind. It will open new per-spectives and unseal the ancient springs to us. Man should lift himself up to God, and not merely to the purposes of his own life. In the same way that life opens itself up and yields the center again, simultaneously and just as intensely it wins its freedom and mastery back. The view for connections and content will be reopened to life, and the earth will be fruit-fully flooded again by the streams of mission, confirmation, and mastery. These are the streams that still carry the ship of life and lead it onward.

This is the first meaning of "Gaudete in Domino". Sepa-rated from the Lord, the whole thing atrophies! We must keep telling people this. It is the most important announce-ment of these days. And we must know it and visibly live it as examples.

With that, we touch upon the second meaning of the Scripture verse: "In Domino—in the Lord." The Lord must and will enkindle anew the light within us, but not only because of natural order or divine precept. *"Dominus propus est—the Lord is near"* tells us He is the God of personal nearness. The theological truths about providence and guidance, about the ever-presence of God, and about His merciful indwelling in us must become concrete, lived possessions. Then we will succeed in living through the experiences and events of workdays and holidays, of bright hours and dark hours, right up to that central point at which God reveals Himself as their deepest meaning. The secret, holy cargo entrusted to these events we are living through consists of His questions, His guidance, His leadership, His punishment, His judgment, His consolation and help. Temples of God are located not only where churches are still standing. Rather, let the great temple arches stretch and raise themselves up wherever the human heart worships, wherever the knee bends, wherever the spirit opens itself, and where man's highest potential is fulfilled by those who worship and love. And finally, may the valiant words of Saint Augustine, Meister Eckhart,[2] and others like them be taken seriously and become lived realities. The life of God is lived within us, within the deepest center of our being. Man becomes truly himself precisely at the point where he recognizes that the highest and brightest Being dwells within him. Moreover, he will rediscover himself and his own identity, as well as his faith in his own individual value, mission, and life options, to the degree that he comprehends human life as streaming forth out of the mystery of God. Then all that is negative and threatening is surmounted, its futility is exposed from within and simultaneously disempowered.

[2] Eckhart von Hochheim, O.P. (approximately 1260–1327), theologian and mystic of the Christian Middle Ages.

Only a person like this will be capable of breathing deeply,[3] and life and the world will not refuse him. They will give all that they rightly have to give, because it is demanded with the sovereign goods of divine jurisdiction, which have been put at his disposal. He will feel the eternal brilliance of creation again, regarding it reverently and protectively. He will award things this intrinsic brilliance again because his mind and heart, his hands and works, have the creative gift and strength to pass the test. And such a person becomes someone of great joy—the great joy that he lives and experiences, as well as gives and enkindles in others. *Gaudete!*

2.

In order for man to attain to this density of life and ascend to this capability of deep breath and deep joy, a great conversion is needed, a great transformation of his being. This will be the result of individual exertion and, equally, the result of a great liberation that God will work in man, to prevent him from locking up and enclosing himself in autarchy, and isolation, and arrogance. The question is, how does man attain to this creative nearness to God that so enables and empowers him?

And the first answer is found once again in the figure of John the Baptist, who personifies Advent. "Et confessus est, et non negavit: Quia non sum ego . . . [And he confessed, and did not deny, I am not He . . .]" (Jn 1:20). Man must be brought to an absolute *clarity about himself* and *honesty before himself* and others. He must come down from all the pedestals of arrogance onto which he always climbs. He must come down from the high horses of vanity and self-deception that,

---

[3] Reference to the Christmas Vigil liturgy: "*Da nobis, quæsumus, Domine . . . respirare—Give us breath, we beseech you, O Lord.*" Compare with "The Blessed Burden", Christmas Vigil, December 24, 1944. —TRANS.

for a time, let themselves be trotted forth so proudly. Finally, though, the horses shy or willfully run away and throw their "master" off in the wilderness—or else they turn out to be miserable nags that someone has curried to a shiny, smooth, and competent appearance.

Sincere modesty, meaning knowledge of boundaries and jurisdiction, as well as a sober insight into the capability and potentiality one has been granted are the first steps to life's truth. "The truth will make you free" (Jn 8:32). After all, the freedom to live a full life is what it is all about.

Man always starts to dream again. There is the authentic, creative dream, the vision that calls us forth from the tired slave's pace of the habitual and usual. Woe, if young people lack vision and their minds are not quickened by the movement of the Holy Spirit! However, there is also a false and foolish dreaming, which obscures the limits of human possibility and reality and conceals them from our consciousness. So instead of expanding his boundaries through sincere watchfulness and authentic exertion, man oversteps them. Overstepping boundaries on the ultimate level of being, however, is deadly.

Two criteria are available to identify whether we are following an authentic impulse or a foolish and presumptuous will-of-the-wisp. Both of these criteria are found in the figure of John the Baptist: service and annunciation.

The voice calling in the wilderness is precisely what it is about: that man remain true to himself and not inflate his own importance. Human honesty requires man to see himself as a servant and perceive his reality as a mission and an assignment. *The idea of authentic service and authentic duty* belongs to the essence of man's self-concept. Anyone who undermines this has smeared his own image and corrupted his own self-knowledge.

Duty and service can take a variety of concrete forms. Here again, though, man can secretly or openly take on displaced priorities and corrupt this clean idea. The second criterion keeps us on track: "Ipse est—He is the One" (Jn 1:27). This calls us to annunciation, testimony, and *praise of the Lord*. Here, man releases himself from all cramps and becomes truly honest and clear sighted. Moreover, an extended personal effort is required to keep giving oneself the impulse to rise above self, to move away from self. But at the same time, this is how man attains the necessary openness in which he must continue if he sincerely wants to strive toward the great realities God has prepared for him.

3.

The honesty with which man should be true to himself is an intrinsic selflessness. Through this selflessness, he should not become a disinterested and uninteresting Nirvanist, but should transcend himself by expressing his openness to God in readiness, service, and praise. *Through this openness he will attain a great freedom,* a freedom from cramps, delusion, and deterioration. Man must travel a great distance before, in that direct encounter with God, he truly and completely finds himself. The distance leads him out beyond himself. It consists of interior preliminaries and experiences, more than externally measurable lengths and distances, although it usually takes many exterior blows from fate before our eyes are opened to the real connections. This need to transcend ourselves is part of man's essence. Otherwise, he would become intellectually bourgeois, pompous, stuffy, ponderous, and comfort loving.

So, make the great gesture toward transcendence? Yes, but differently. Not as degenerate and degenerating arrogance, but rather as an honest self-realization of our nature. Human nature is so firmly established that it has imprinted the traces of its true strength and structure even upon man's decadence. Precisely where man most dangerously errs in deluded and autarkical arrogance, in hubris and proud stupidity, dreaming of a master race, and so forth, he also reveals the essential human vocation: he must be more than human, if he wants to become and remain human. Anyone who wants to be merely human and nothing else—and knows nothing more about himself than the human dailinesses and daily human-nesses—will soon vegetate into something subhuman. And that is the metaphysical reason for the present human crisis on our continent.

Here again, man must remain honest in this regard. Great freedom cannot be gained by robbery. Freedom is encounter, not contrariness, rebellion, or arrogance. The fires of Prometheus are mythological fires. The heavenly powers are strong and wise enough to protect what is their own. They have no need of ridiculous, gruesome gestures of revenge to reveal and document their strength and jurisdiction.[4] God does not seek revenge. He is simply Himself, and anyone who denies this is loading himself with burdens beneath which he will collapse.

What man contributes to his great liberation into a fulfilled life consists of honest humility, willing openness, readiness to serve, authentic testimony, and praise. If man sets out upon this Advent road, he will be granted the great encounter, for man's liberation happens as an encounter. God works a multifaceted liberation within him, meeting him when he rises beyond self in a lived personal experience of being comforted and uplifted.

[4] According to the Greek myth, Prometheus stole fire from Zeus and gave it to mankind. Zeus took revenge, chaining Prometheus to a rock, where an eagle came daily to feed on his liver. The punishment was endless because the liver continually grew back. —TRANS.

"Benedixisti . . . terram tuam [et] avertisti captivitatem. . . . Excita . . . potentiam tuam, et veni. [You have blessed . . . Your land and averted captivity. . . . Awaken . . . Your power and come]." (See the Third Sunday Introit and First and Fourth Sunday Collect, Offertory, and Postcommunion Prayer.) These all testify to God's intervention for the benefit of mankind. They include the recognition of man's basic human situation, with which man must first come to terms.

This situation consists of man's absolute powerlessness in connection with the ultimate experiences and fulfillment. The liturgy calls this powerlessness "captivitas—imprisonment" and "iniquitas—guilt". Man will become capable of ultimate self-realization only through an intervention by God, who breaks open the prison, who cancels the debt and brings a blessing. How man got into this condition is totally beside the point. It is only interesting, in a disturbing and upsetting way, that the Church goes along with the present helpless, shoulder-shrugging attitude of modern society toward these ultimate questions and possibilities. Nevertheless, the consequences are different and curative, while dwelling on the actual powerlessness only makes the evil situation even worse and more hopeless.

Man often feels every step newly ensnares his foot in some kind of thicket, from which he will never get out. To the close observer, the depressing fact reveals itself that human beings have limitations imposed upon them that are harder, narrower, and more impassable than the limitations of nature. *Imprisonment* is what the liturgy terms this state, *related to iniquitas—guilt*. We often use the word imprisonment, but you need to have endured it yourself in order to know what it says about the inner being. You need to have sat in a small room with your hands in irons and have seen the shredded flag of freedom standing in the corner, in a thousand images of melancholy. The heart flees from these images again and again, and the mind strives to lift itself free, only to awaken even more sharply to reality at the next guard's footsteps sounding in the hall and the next clanking of keys. Then you know that you are powerless. You have no key, and your door has no inner keyhole, and your window is barred and set so high that you cannot even look out. If no one comes and releases you, you will remain bound and poor in misery. All the mental struggles do not help at all. This is a fact, a condition that exists and must be acknowledged.

Well now, this is the condition of human beings today. That is to say, the reason man has become so poor, damaged, and incapable of managing life is that God's liberation has not come to him. Just as I know that only the Lord God can and will loose my fetters and open my door, and that only His creative storm will unfurl my flag once again, exactly the same thing applies to man. But for him to have the right insight into these circumstances, he needs to call upon our redeeming God persistently and to wait in openness. God's salvation does not abuse and violate us. We must keep telling people these days that the Lord stands ready and waiting at the gates. The entire bitter course of events is not only a judgment, but should be taken just as seriously as God Himself hammering on the gates of our minds, our spirits, and our freedom, for us to surrender them to Him.

By ourselves and with our own strength *alone*, we will *not* manage it. The theological principle that a man, by his own strength, cannot even sustain the basic ethical level of natural principles[5] is the rationale for the misery that we are living through today.

[5] Christian theology defines the relationship between grace and nature such that, even for the fulfillment of the natural moral laws, the assistance of grace is necessary.

Man is challenged again to stand and deliver. Only, he does not merely exchange one set of fetters for another. God's calls are always creative. They increase the very reality within us that is called upon, precisely because of their realness and authenticity.

Therefore, our own lives absolutely, urgently, and immediately need an ongoing conversion and abandonment to God, so that His will to save us can become redeemingly, creatively effective. We must begin this immediately and keep on with it.

Occidental man is suffocating. This is not limited merely to personal existence, the personal earthly and heavenly salvation of the individual. For the sake of the future of the world and the praise it should offer to God, it is critical that the Occident attains freedom of land and sea once again.

Need I add that all of this requires the existence and development of the capability for joy? Need I add that only such a person will have a sense, a feel, a look at the innermost realities?

Freedom is the breath of life. We sit in musty bomb cellars and cramped prisons and groan under the bursting and destructive blows of fate. We should finally stop giving everything a false glamour and unrealistic value and begin to bear it for what it is—unredeemed life. As soon as we do this, the jangling of chains and the trembling of nerves and the faintness of heart transform themselves into a litany: "Rorate cæli . . . [Drop down, dew . . .]." We should much more definitively unite our concrete destiny with these connections and call upon God's redeeming freedom. Then the narrowness widens, our lungs breathe in fresh air again, and the horizon has promises again. Existence still weeps and mourns, but already a soft, joyous melody of longing and knowledge is ringing through the broken voices of the mourners.[6]

4.

With this knowledge and this attitude, man releases himself from the unmediated relationship to things and conditions. He finds himself at a wholesome and healing distance—not the goal-oriented and cool distance of calculation, organization, mechanization, but rather that higher level of freedom, the perspective given to someone looking down from the heights at what lies below. The voice of such a person is not so quickly silenced.

"Nihil sollciti sitis [Do not worry about anything]" (Phil 4:6). That is how the Epistle identifies this freedom that releases man from the harassment of the driven days, the counted hours, the vibrating fear. Everything is clearly visible; the greater connections are known and, above all, the place is recognized—the only place where binding appraisal takes place and ultimate decisions are made. This place is the point at which God's creative and healing freedom meets man's seeking and calling freedom. Our distress does not die there, but the worry does. The burden does not disappear, but the faintheartedness does. The assignment and the testing of our existence continue there, but not as a torturing concern.

"Innotescant apud Deum. [Make your requests known to God]" (Phil 4:6). Man knows the center of his existence has shifted over into God. Paul reminds us here of some fundamental attitudes appropriate to those who want to find themselves. One who loves, for example, is an original and basic

---

[6] Compare this passage with the final paragraph of "Figures of Advent" (p. 30). —TRANS.

human model. One who is reverent is equally a model. Paul adds to these the models of gratitude, of worship, and of supplication. Someone who has centered his life in the truly appropriate relationship with God effects a personal, I–Thou connection.[7] Such a person can find himself at last, because he has just properly begun to be. And in the consummation of this life, long-lost or atrophied capabilities begin to grow or to reawaken. The substance expands, and the eyes become brighter and keener. A new confidence and certainty stay with him, even through times of shaking and quaking. Still under way, still in suspense and tribulation, still facing trial and testing, but indeed man is over the worst. The soul knows songs again and hears the secret springs flowing again. It makes a breakthrough toward the realization of "joy in the Lord", and one day this soul will sing the old jubilant song, praising the blessed encounter—*Alleluia!*

5.

All this holds true and will happen to the extent that man decides to be willingly open and receptive. But it happens and applies, in accordance to our limitations as creatures, in a *reticent manner*, which is the only way man can bear God's reality and happiness. This partial vision is sufficient radiant happiness for anyone who feels and knows and believes. Yet this is just the first beginning, the pledge, idea, and first breath. The "ever-greater" and "always-still-more" of eternity is shimmering through all the cracks of creation and keeping life in a state of dynamic urgency.

In this way, life attains to its farthest horizon, and the

[7] A relationship where dialogue is possible, the *I–Thou relationship*, as defined in the book *Ich und Du* (*I and Thou*) by Martin Buber (Leipzig: Insel Verlag, 1923). —TRANS.

moment attains its fullest resonance: the *promises* are always calling us. This is a wonderful word from Isaiah in the communion verse: "Announce: 'You faint-hearted ones . . .'" (Is 35:4). Speak to all creation and touch the deepest wounds of reality with healing and comfort. Woe, when a life, a world, a people have no more promises! Because that means they have no more life, no splendor, no confidence, no courage, and no happiness. Joy dies.

The promises of God stand above us, more valid than the stars and more effective than the sun. Based on these promises, we will become healthy and free, from the center of our being. The promises have turned us around and, at once, opened life out into the infinite. Even lamentation retains the song of these promises, and distress their sound, and loneliness their confidence.

Well, what about the joy whose message we await, the joy we want to become initiated in and capable of? Have I said anything about the manifold and exciting joys that can be experienced in the shining of the sun, in the movement of the waters, in the blooming of flowers, in a meeting with a true friend? Have I said anything about the joyful emotions that can mean that man experiences real love and real suffering, or how Heaven and earth can be occasions of great and deep joy?

I have said nothing about these. I know perfectly well the many sources from which joy can flow out to man—and that all these sources also can fall silent. That is not what it's about. It's about that old theme of my life: man becomes healthy through the order of God and in nearness to God. That is also where he becomes capable of joy and happiness. Establishing the order of God, and announcing God's nearness, and teaching it and bringing it to others: that is what my life means and wants, and what it is sworn to and abides by.

Week IV

Our hearts must become strong,
to make the divine heartbeat
into the law of life again.

— Alfred Delp, S.J.
  Pre-Christmas Reflection, 1942

Liturgy for the Fourth Sunday of Advent

Introit: Isaiah 45:8, Psalm 19:1(18:2)

Rorate, cæli, desuper, et nubes pluant justum: aperiatur terra, et germinet Salvatorem. Cæli enarrant gloriam Dei: et opera manuum ejus annuntiat firmamentum. Gloria Patri, et Filio, et Spiritui Sancto. Sicut erat in principio, et nunc, et semper, et in sæcula sæculorum. Amen.

Drop down, dew from heaven above, and let the clouds rain down the Just One. Let the earth open and blossom forth a Savior. The heavens reveal God's glory: and the skies announce the work of His hands. Glory be to the Father, and to the Son, and to the Holy Spirit. As it was in the beginning, is now, and ever shall be, world without end. Amen.

Collect:

Excita, quæsumus, Domine, potentiam tuam, et veni: et magna nobis virtute succurre; ut per auxilium gratiæ tuæ, quod nostra peccata præpediunt, indulgentia tuæ propitiationis acceleret: Qui vivis et regnas cum Deo Patre in unitate Spiritus Sancti, Deus, per omnia sæcula sæculorum. Amen.

Awaken Your power, we beseech You, O Lord, and come! With Your great strength hasten to assist us, so that the salvation that is hindered by our sins will be speedily granted us through Your mercy, who live and reign with God the Father in the unity of the Holy Spirit, God, for ever and ever. Amen.

Epistle: 1 Corinthians 4:1–5

Fratres: Sic nos existimet homo ut ministros Christi, et dispensatores mysteriorum Dei. Hic jam quæritur inter dispensatores, ut fidelis quis inveniatur. Mihi autem pro minimo est, ut a vobis judicer aut ab humano die: sed neque meipsum judico. Nihil enim mihi conscius sum: sed non in hoc justificatus sum: qui autem judicat me, Dominus est. Itaque nolite ante tempus judicare, quoadusque veniat Dominus: qui et illuminabit abscondita tenebrarum, et manifestabit consilia cordium: et tunc laus erit unicuique a Deo.

Brethren: Let us be seen as servants of Christ and administrators of the mysteries of God. Now, of administrators, it is expected that they will be found to be faithful. It is nothing to me to be judged by you or by a human tribunal. I do not even judge myself. I am not conscious of anything, but I am not yet therefore justified. The One who judges me is the Lord. Therefore, judge not before the time, before the Lord comes. He will bring to light the hidden things of darkness and will reveal the intentions of hearts. They will each receive praise accordingly from God.

Gradual: Psalm 145(144):18, 21

Prope est Dominus omnibus invocantibus eum: omnibus qui invocant eum in veritate.
V. Laudem Domini loquetur os meum: et benedicat omnis caro nomen sanctum ejus.

The Lord is near to all who call upon Him, to all who call upon Him in truth.
V. My mouth shall speak the praise of the Lord. Let all flesh bless His holy name.

Alleluia:

Allelulia, alleluia.
V. Veni, Domine, et noli tardare: relaxa facinora plebis tuæ Israël.
Alleluia.

Alleluia, alleluia.
V. Come, O Lord, and do not delay. Lift the weight of the
burden of sin from Your people Israel. Alleluia.

Gospel: Luke 3:1–6

Anno quintodecimo imperii Tiberii Cæsaris, procurante Pontio
Pilato Judæam, tetrarcha autem Galilææ Herode, Philippo autem
fratre ejus tetrarcha Ituræœ et Trachonitidis regionis, et Lysania
Abilinæ tetrarcha, sub principibus sacerdotum Anna et Caipha:
factum est verbum Domini super Joannem, Zachariæ filium, in
deserto. Et venit in omnem regionem Jordanis, prædicans baptismum
pænitentiæ in remissionem peccatorum, sicut scriptum est in libro
sermonum Isaiæ prophetæ: Vox clamantis in deserto: Parate viam
Domini: rectas facite semitas ejus: omnis vallis implebitur: et omnis
mons, et collis humiliabitur: et erunt prava in directa, et aspera in vias
planas: et videbit omnis caro salutare Dei.

In the fifteenth year of the reign of Tiberius Caesar, as
Pontius Pilate was governor of Judea, and Herod was tetrarch
of Galilee, and Philip his brother was tetrarch of Ituraea and
the country of Trachonitis, and Lysanias was tetrarch of
Abilene, under the high priests Annas and Caiphas: the word
of the Lord came to John the son of Zachary, in the desert.
And he came into all the country around the Jordan, preaching the baptism of penance for the remission of sins; as it is
written in the book of the prophet Isaiah: The voice of one
crying in the wilderness, "Prepare the way of the Lord, make

straight His paths. Every valley shall be filled, and every mountain and hill shall be leveled. The crooked ways shall be made straight and the rough ways smooth. And all flesh shall see the salvation of God."

Offertory: Luke 1:28, 42

Ave, Maria, gratia plena: Dominus tecum: benedicta tu in mulieribus, et benedictus fructus ventris tui.

Hail, Mary, full of grace. The Lord is with you. You are blessed among women, and blessed is the fruit of your womb.

Secret:

Sacrificiis præsentibus, quæsumus, Domine, placatus intende: ut et devotioni nostræ proficiant et saluti. Per Dominum nostrum Jesum Christum, Filium tuum, qui tecum vivit et regnat in unitate Spiritus Sancti, Deus, per omnia sæcula sæculorum. Amen.

Receive these sacrifices favorably, O Lord, we beseech You, that they may increase our devotion and lead us to salvation. Through our Lord Jesus Christ, Your Son, who lives and reigns with You in the unity of the Holy Spirit, God, for ever and ever. Amen.

Communion: Isaiah 7:14

Ecce, Virgo concipiet et pariet filium: et vocabitur nomen ejus Emmanuel.

See, a virgin will conceive and give birth to a son, and His name will be Emmanuel (*God with us*).

Postcommunion:

Sumptis muneribus, quæsumus, Domine: ut, cum frequentatione mysterii, crescat nostræ salutis effectus. Per Dominum nostrum Jesum Christum, Filium tuum, qui tecum vivit et regnat in unitate Spiritus Sancti, Deus, per omnia sæcula sæculorum. Amen.

Having received your gifts, we beseech You, O Lord, that our recourse to this sacrament may work toward our salvation. Through our Lord Jesus Christ, Your Son, who lives and reigns with You in the unity of the Holy Spirit, God, for ever and ever. Amen.

Homily for the Fourth Sunday of Advent
Preached in Munich
December 21, 1941

"And all flesh shall see the salvation of God" (Lk 3:6). This final sentence of today's Gospel promises the very thing we have comprehended as the meaning of Advent and man's fundamental Advent attitude, that is, the personal encounter with the Lord, with the Absolute. Yet before that happens, a fourth Advent-call rings out, a fourth call to mankind, to our very being. It is a call to bring reality into the order it should be in, if we want to meet the Lord and if we really are practicing Advent—which means being under way, seeking, and waiting.

Advent has already called man three times. It called through the shaking; it called to authenticity; and it called to confession of faith. And now Advent calls a fourth time. Without this fourth call, the other three are not possible. They are just pathos; they are talk; they are gestures and rhetoric; but they are not genuine and do not stem from the final reality within us. This fourth Advent call signifies a fundamental attitude of man. It is an old term, a forgotten word, and a forgotten value: *fear of God*.

When I say "fear" of God, there is one thing I do not mean. I do not mean being afraid of God. There is no greater parody and no greater caricature of the meaning of religion than wanting to build a religion upon fear. There is no

greater injustice to God the Lord than the calculated trembling and timidity of a slave or a dog, the cowardly fear of a
person who expects to lose something or who feels threatened by some kind of danger that might come upon him
from this God. No, fear of God expresses, first of all—and
this old meaning should be rediscovered—that God is the
Lord. How does it go in today's Epistle for Sunday? "It is
nothing to me to be judged by you or by a human tribunal. I
do not even judge myself. I am not conscious of anything,
but I am not yet therefore justified. The One who judges me
is the Lord" (1 Cor 4:3–4).

Man must learn again—really, personally, practically, and
daily—to reckon with God as the ultimate category of reality,
as the decisive judgment of all that exists. Saint Paul stands
there and says to both his friends and his foes, "I don't care
whether you judge me. I fear no human tribunal. Even in the
area where people are the mightiest, where they are able to
stand in judgment and destroy; I don't care. I don't care,
either, that I have nothing to reproach myself for." Even in
the area where an individual possesses his greatest certainty
and greatest justification, his own conscience—even there,
Paul remains silent. He steps back and says: "Even there, you
have to ask the one and only Lord."

We have lost this category. We are no longer a people of
clarity who know about this one Lord and who stand in
simplicity, without usurping the Lord's rights, without be-
traying our duty to Him, or bargaining. We have become a
people of many lords, somehow divided, somehow sepa-
rated. We could use more than two hands to make it all come
out right and make it good. Fear of God does not mean being
afraid. It does not mean slavish cowardice or breaking down
before God the Lord. Rather, it means knowing the absolute,
inalienable dominion of the Lord of all. Much in our lives

would be different if more people knew the easy, simple sentence—and vividly understood—that God is the Lord.

For anyone who comprehends the fear of God in this way, not only does the slavish fear of God die, but the anxious fear of other people dies as well. In the Gospel, once again and for the third time, this hard and austere figure of the man from the wilderness, John the Baptist, stands before us. And before he and his message are discussed, before his boldness is mentioned, there are a couple of names. They indicate the historical moment within which John is called.[1]

It says here: "In the fifteenth year of the reign of Tiberius Caesar . . ." (Lk 3:1–2). This was the Roman emperor. This was the co-regent and heir of Augustus. This was the man who, to secure his own power, granted his predecessor more and more divine honors, because he knew that reverence for an emperor who is dead implies reverence for the emperor who is alive. It did not take long until the first temple for that emperor-god stood in Smyrna. Moreover, it did not take long for the cowardly populace to understand and for the cities to decide humbly to ask permission to build temples to the divine emperor.

"In the fifteenth year of the reign of the Emperor Tiberius, as Pontius Pilate was governor of Judea . . ." Pontius Pilate. This was the man who had Christ scourged and crucified. This was the man against whom a formal complaint was written to Caesar from Judea: "Your governor is a gruesome, unscrupulous, obstinate man. He is corrupt and predatory; he violates honor and abuses the people. He is executing countless people without a trial. The atrocities have become unbearable." Pontius Pilate. This was a man

---

[1] In the description of personalities and events that follows, Fr. Delp's listeners would have recognized his intended parallels to recent events (see Chronology, 1941). —TRANS.

who wanted the world. When he wanted to build an aque-
duct, he decided that money in the Synagogues was uselessly
lying around. This was the man who ordered the emperor's
image set up in the sacred space; and this was the man who
had only one priority in his life: to remain a friend of Caesar.
When once, during his meeting with the true Lord, his conscience began to vibrate softly, and he began to lose something of his forceful certainty, it was enough to remind him:
"Friend of Caesar, your friendship is in danger!" Then, like a
desert jackal, all was forgotten, and our Lord went to the
Cross.

". . . As Pontius Pilate was governor of Judea, as Herod
was tetrarch of Galilee . . ." Herod. This was the son of a
profligate father, the son of a man with nine wives, whose
father wasted all his energy on his passions, including the one
boundless passion that his sons inherited. Herod was a sly,
self-indulgent hedonist. He knew only one thing: how to
follow his impulses. He took everything spiritual, everything
higher, everything good, and everything of ultimate value,
and exchanged these things for total turbidity and blindness
in all his senses.

". . . And as his brother Philip was tetrarch of Ituraea and
Trachonitis . . ." Herod's brother Philip was an innocuous
type, harmless, not dangerous, but hooked on foreign traditions. He betrayed his people through foreign rights,
foreign morals, and foreign customs. Nothing could be expected from him by anyone who might arise as prophet in
Israel.

". . . And as Lysanias was tetrarch of Abilene . . ." Lysanias,
whose name faded and died away, was the little-known heir
and descendant of a well-known father. From the great kingdom of old Lysanias, a small shred still remained. He was a
harmless and unremarkable man, who presented no danger,

but could not be expected to protect human rights, his people, or the civil order.

And then it says here: "under the high priests Annas and Caiaphas", and that tells us that, not only was there no hope from worldly power, the holy place was also sold out. There was Annas, a rich man. He was high priest for nine years and, afterward, he bought the office year after year for his family of five sons. And then his son-in-law, Caiaphas, this back-stabbing, gruesome, hard-hearted fellow, who had discovered one thing: religion as a means to power. He suffocated everything religious that affected his power.

That was the historical situation, that was the hour, and that was the world into which John stepped. But here it says: "The Word of the Lord came to John . . . in the desert" (Lk 3:2).

The Word of the Lord! In such times, one must be motivated, not from willfulness, or personal whim, or personal programs, but really from the very heart and center of reality after having subjected oneself to God the Lord and wrestled with His Word. Then such a person will touch the minds of those who ask and beg for the word, for the instruction, for the insight to cope with this historical time and situation— and with the distress, and with the yearning, and the darkness and all the unspeakable things. He will truly enkindle a fervor and frenzy in these souls. But then they must subject themselves to the Word of the Lord and stand by it. They must stand, not make bargains as if it were hopeless, and not be silent as if it were hopeless.

Think of it: Tiberius, Pontius Pilate, Herod, Philip, Lysanias, Annas, Caiaphas. When was there a more hopeless hour?

And then the Word of the Lord came to John. The Word of the Lord! This is the second aspect of the fear of God. The fear of other people disappears. Anxiety, that unworthy, inner subversion of mankind, fades away.

There is also a third aspect to the fear of God. We find it in the Word of the Lord to John, as John proclaimed it. He preached the baptism of repentance and the forgiveness of sins, the great metanoia, the great return to God (Lk 3:3). Continually, continually, that old arrogance wafts through the world, causing people all at once to discover, "I am somebody." All at once, people discover their own style, their own worth, their own intellectual space to talk, and they have to live all that out. "I am who I am." You only have to say that once out loud, and you notice what lies behind it. I AM WHO AM. Long ago, that was said as the Lord unveiled Himself in the flames of fire and revealed Himself to the people as leader, as lawgiver, as ὁ ὤν, He Who Is. I AM WHO AM (Ex 3:14). And He is the only one who is unique and ultimate. He alone has the right to say, "Here is uniqueness that is lived out, and that must be lived." In His presence, the other voices fall silent. He is the standard of measurement, and, therefore, man's life is this ongoing metanoia, this ongoing genuine conversion.

Let us not make of penance the couple of tiny feelings that get pinched when we count up a couple of trifles, while remaining unshaken in our fundamental attitudes, striding through the world like gods and never noticing that with each breath we commit a worse sin. That sin is arrogance: puffing ourselves up and not submitting ourselves to God the Lord. This is why the believer, the person who has seen God, is so totally different, so totally other—because our God is totally Other, with a fullness and order different from what the world sees at first glance. Further, someone who observes the otherness of the believer will be changed by it. Out of this metanoia, this spiritual switching-over and transformation of being, comes the marked foreign quality of the Christian. Yet from this same source comes certitude, an intrinsic, resilient *unshaken*-ness as well. This comes from knowing he is master of the situation and of all things, because of being truly in contact with the center of reality.

These have been our reflections on man in Advent, in the encounter with the Absolute:

—being shaken, in the experience of quaking,
—in authenticity, in ultimate integrity,
—in confession of faith, and
—in this forthright and realistic fear of the Lord.

Believe me, if someone comes out of an encounter with the Absolute in any other way, then he is blind. So much remains veiled from him, and the promise remains silent. No Christmas star will rise, no Christmas candles will glow, and no Christmas bells will ring out. So much remains mute, cold, gruesome, violent. That letter about Pontius Pilate almost describes the lives of people who live without Advent, without homecoming, without journeying—people who stand without reality before the Lord. "All flesh shall see the salvation of God" (Lk 3:6): yes, all of us who are under way on this journey, and open ourselves and are really working for salvation.

Pre-Christmas Reflection
Preached in Munich
December 22, 1942

The meaning of our Christian holy days is not primarily our external holiday celebration, but that particular mysteries of God happen to us, and that we respond. Something in the deepest center of our being is meant here, more than the exterior symbols can even indicate. Anyone who lacks spiritual eyes, and whose soul has not become open and watchful, will not understand the reason we are so often festive in the cycle of the liturgical year. The Church stands before us with great gestures and great pomp and ceremonial rites. This is only an attempt to indicate something that reaches much deeper and must be taken much more seriously.

We need to celebrate holy days in three ways. First, by recalling a historical event. The feasts are always based on verifiable, historical facts. We should not just get carried away with unbridled enthusiasm. What is really going on? This is a question of discernment and recognition. Seen from God's perspective, there is always a clearly defined event connected to the mystery, a clear statement intended, a fact.

This brings us to the second point. Within all of the foregoing, a great mystery—the *Mysterium*—is hidden. Something happens between Heaven and earth that passes all understanding. This mystery is made present to us, continues in the world till the end of time, and is always in the process of happening—the abiding *Mysterium*.

These two points are followed by the third way in which we must consider the feast to be serious and important. Through the historical facts and through the workings of the mystery, the holy day simultaneously issues a challenge to each individual life, a message that demands a particular attitude and an interior decision from each person to whom it is proclaimed.

The Christmas celebration is the birth of the Lord. It is verifiable that Christ was born on this night. The great mystery behind this is the marriage covenant of God with mankind; that mankind is fulfilled only insofar as it has grown into this covenant. Concretely, it is meaningful to establish what this covenant, which began between divinity and humanity on that Holy Night, signifies as a challenge and message for each one of us.

In view of these preconditions, we want to read some passages from the Holy Scriptures about the mystery of Christmas—the three readings of the three Christmas Masses.

1. The Epistle for the Third Christmas Mass: "In many and various ways God spoke in times past to our fathers through the prophets; but in these last days He has spoken to us through a Son, whom He appointed the heir of the cosmos, through whom also He created the world. He reflects the glory of God and bears the very stamp of His nature, upholding the universe by His Word of power" (Heb 1:1–3). Basically, before moving on to personal devotions and contemplation or reading stories of the Holy Night, one should read these weighty verses of Saint Paul to be spiritually touched by the impact of this holy day we are celebrating. We Germans run the risk of concealing Christmas behind bourgeois customs and sentimentality, behind all those traditions that make this holiday dear and precious to us. Yet

perhaps the deep meaning is still hiding behind all those things. What this celebration is about is the founding of a final order for the world, a new center of meaning for all existence. We are not celebrating some children's holiday, but rather the fact that God has spoken His ultimate Word to the world. Christ is the ultimate Word of God to the world. One must let this idea really sink in these days when people are seeking new values. If you take God seriously—this relationship between God and the world—and if you know how important God is to society as well as to private life, then this has to touch you. The ultimate Word of God to the world! God does not contradict Himself and does not repeat Himself. One must use every ounce of willpower to comprehend this, and let this concept sink in: Christ, as the ultimate Word of God to the world.

And Christ came and placed Himself before us as a message. That He came as a child proves how much it matters to God that the message be accepted. From this Holy Night onward, the world has had the possibility of living in nearness to God or living apart from God. The entire Epistle wants to communicate one thing: take this, take what has happened here, really seriously. What came into the world is the very image of the Divine Being, is God Himself. He lifted mankind out of every false order in this consecrated night, in this blessed night. What is said to us here gives life its meaning, individual life as well as the life of all mankind.

The ultimate Word of God to mankind. This idea is expanded upon as follows:

2. The Epistle of the Second Mass of Christmas: "The goodness and kindness of God our Savior appeared; He saved us, not because of deeds done by us in righteousness, but by virtue of His own mercy" (Tit 3:4–7). The impact of these facts is further developed in two ways. What does this mean

for man's inner reality, where he must come to an under-standing of himself? And what does it mean for the funda-mental attitudes toward life, the point at which the mystery becomes present and calls for a concrete response? To begin with the first question: What has happened to the measure of our being, through this Word that God has spoken into the world? The goodness and loving-kindness of God have ap-peared, so that we know and seriously must recognize our-selves as the substance of a divine commitment to man. Since then, God has taken no other position in relation to us than this "benignitas et humanitas [goodness and loving-kindness]". Because God's commitment upholds each and every one of us, even to the extent of His sharing in the very poorest and most helpless phase of human infancy, He has fully realized and made Himself accessible in the Incarnation. And now, in the background, our great, gruesome time stands up.

"Not because of deeds done by us in righteousness, but by virtue of His own mercy" (Tit 3:5). The second thing we need to know is that it is not because man is proud and worthy, but because God upholds us. Man needs to know that we live from grace; we live from God's merciful com-mitment to mankind, from His mercy. Not as miserable wretches, however, but renewed in spirit; so that we know our intrinsic dignity, know that we are raised up above and beyond all else, because we mean so much to God. This is how we attain maturity in the presence of God.

3. Now—in the Epistle of the First Mass of Christmas—the effect of the foregoing is described. We will not be abused and violated, not even forced to be good or forced to love. We are challenged to do so, but it calls for a decision. The grace of God our Savior "teaches us to renounce godlessness and to live moral, upright, and pious lives in this world" (Tit

2:12). There are three great fundamental attitudes there, three great, foreign qualities of Christians in the world, three great commandments for perfection of life.

First [renouncing godlessness]: if the meaning of our lives is that God is really in covenant with mankind, then there can be no more godlessness—that would be loss of being—there is no more will to live. Godlessness is a calumniation of the divine life.

Second [regarding moral, upright, and godly living]: man should recognize that his innermost purpose is to find the way home to God and to be caught up in His life, to seek God for Himself. The fundamental concept of man in this world never can be that of certainty, but rather that of waiting for this ultimate revelation of that which began in the Holy Night. Such people, who know they are hastening to meet a great fulfillment, are always people under way.

Third [to become His own followers]:[1] these are people of loneliness, the people whom God wanted to have as His people, gripped by a great passion that God be well pleased, and ablaze with the divine fire that will be cast upon the earth.

And now, here is the last question: What does all of this mean today—the message of the great *Kyrios*, the Lord, the message of the fundamental attitude that the Holy Night demands? This is no Christmas life today. Neither is it a Christmas life according to people's inner attitude. Neither is

[1] The context of Tit 2:12 clarifies Fr. Delp's point. The complete text, translated from the Latin, reads: "The grace of God our Savior has appeared to all mankind. It teaches us to renounce godlessness and the worldly passions, and to live sober, upright, and godly lives in this world. Meanwhile, we await, in blessed hope, the glorious coming of our great God and Savior, Jesus Christ, who gave Himself up for us to redeem us from all iniquity and to purify us so that we become His own: a people who are pleasing to Him, who follow in good works" (Tit 2:11–15). —TRANS.

it a Christmas holy day according to a religious perspective. The world is hostile and rejects everything. But we are experiencing the other side of Christmas. All of these blessings have already been taken away, and the night has descended again.

The first message is that the *Kyrios,* the Lord, is coming. The Lord does not stand in the center anymore. He is replaced by the power brokers. How man keeps lapsing into heresy! The power brokers, under whose power man has gone astray, stand in the center. One no longer sees God as the center of the world, as the foundational support. And what has developed out of this? We are standing without any foundation—we have nothing permanent anymore. There is no more talk of man's life being dependent upon mercy. Therefore the world has become so unmerciful. When has anyone taken away more from man than this? This is a time in which "apparuit benignitas et humanitas [the goodness and loving-kindness of God our Savior appearing]" is no longer acknowledged. What has become of man, that he does not want to be human in relation to God anymore? Beforehand, the Christmas words were sent packing.[2] This is a world in which it no longer can be said that "we await the great revelation of the Lord", a world that must cling to each day because it already knows that, in mere seconds, everything can be over. There is nothing left of peace and security. This is a world that no longer knows of the Holy Night, of the Consecration-Night, the Christ-Mass.[3] That is the one thing that we honestly have to see. The world in which we stand is

[2] References are to Nazi regulations restricting or forbidding Christian practice and customs. —TRANS.

[3] The German word for Christmas is *Weihnacht,* but Fr. Delp wrote "*Weihe-Nacht*" (Consecration-Night). Compare "Meditation for the Fourth Sunday of Advent, 1944", note 13, p. 151. —TRANS.

un-Christmaslike, not because God is unmerciful, but rather because man has outlawed the message, and there is no room anymore for the promise.

Nevertheless, we must also look at this in a positive way. For us personally, this message of the Holy Night still does contain its great meaning and content. There are two things we need to have in terms of consciousness and attitude, and we should take possession of them today: we should not come to Midnight Mass as if we do not live in the year 1942. The year must be redeemed along with everything else. And from the Gloria, we have to take with us the peace and faith in the glory of God. There is nothing else that surpasses this night, and nothing that should be taken as more important than this event. Whatever may happen around us, let us not break down, for then we would not be taking the Lord seriously, or what we know about consecrated people seriously, or what we know about these messages. Therefore, deep down, we are the people who are comforted; and we are the last refuge for the homeless people who do not know anything about the Lord anymore. May we know about the indisputable fact of this Child and not let ourselves be disconcerted, not even by our own great un-freedom. "Apparuit benignitas et humanitas [the goodness and loving-kindness of God our Savior appearing]" (Tit 3:4). That should find its expression in the positive attitudes we take with us from this experience of the Holy Night. May we impart the goodness. May we attend to humanity again, and witness to the Lordship of God again, and know of His grace and mercy, and have gentle hands for other people again. And may we go away from Christmas Eve with the consolation that we mean so much to God that no external distress can rob us of this ultimate consolation. Our hearts must become strong, to make the divine heartbeat into the law of life again. God's readiness is established, but our gates are locked.

These should be the meaning of our wartime Christmas:

—that we petition Him,
—that He redeems us through the mystery,
—that we are rich and capable enough through God's comfort to give mankind the comfort that it needs so much,
—that we go away from this celebration as the great comforters, as the great knowers, the great blessed ones who know what it means to be consoled by God.

Meditation for the Fourth Sunday of Advent
Written in Tegel Prison, Berlin
December 1944

Threefold Bondage and Liberation

The same thing applies to the Advent of prayer as to the Advent of life. All hopes and all hindrances are rolled together into one great weight just before the veil lifts. Before our perspective widens and reveals the fullness of reality, we enter into an experience where all is veiled and dark. Life is like this now more than ever, and especially our lives. Yet at the same time, the fervent confidence, the pressing expectation, and the rightfulness of the promise gather themselves together into one great victorious impulse. Day will be victorious and will compel night to acknowledge its powerlessness and to be downgraded to a demonic-but-powerless facade, or to be transformed into a temple of light. The liturgical readings for the Fourth Sunday of Advent gather together one more time everything that is veiled, and all that hinders us, for a great and ultimate introduction of light.[1] This is a final offer that recognizes our fetters and hopelessness; and yet, it already senses and feels and assures us of the flowing power of the creative graces to come.

[1] Rev 22:5: "And there will be no more night. They will need no light from lamps or the sun, for the Lord will be their light. . . ." —TRANS.

The Threefold Law of Fetters

The Law of Guilt

"Quod nostra peccata præpediunt: salvation that is still hindered by our sins" (Collect). This sets aside the whole jargon of destiny, and so on, the whole passive response to misfortune and to life being shaken. This unites the road through the night, which we must travel, to the important decisions of our hearts. We have to take this consideration seriously. It applies to all those processes that begin with a decision favoring the night of arrogance and self-will. It applies to all times, eras, and generations for whom the old precept applies: "Salvation and destruction arrive by means of the same road." Wrong decisions of the heart and blindness of the mind[2] curse the hands to wretched, destructive actions; and the opposite also holds true. The metanoia of the heart brings about the enlightenment of reflection and return to God, the consecration to healing and blessed work.

That also applies to our personal lives. These events in which we are caught up are interwoven in two ways. The first is that of a general historical causality, the logical connectedness of apparently inevitable necessity. Yet the other existential connectedness, with its aim of trial and testing, the purification and sanctification of our personal lives, is much more final and conclusive. It is here in this existential and personal significance and willingness that the decision about the value or lack of value of our experiences lies. This is where man is given power over every destiny. At this point of the innermost reality of the facts, a door opens to the bright

---

[2] Compare with: "The lord of this world has blinded their minds to keep them from seeing the light of the Gospel of the glory of Christ" (2 Cor 4:4). —TRANS.

room of meaning. Destiny loses its power as soon as we make sense of it. And here, too, man has the power to strike hard, cold, cruel stone and compel redeeming and refreshing springs to gush forth.[3]

We absolutely must find and proclaim this recognition and these connections today. Our life has become hard and harmful to an extent that far exceeds the natural measure of hardship and distress that were always part of life. The causes are gruesome cruelty and obstructed, fettered salvation. The liberation must begin with the great conversion—the silent transformation of hearts that happens in the fruitful silence necessary to all authentic transformation—which, gathering itself to a mighty strength, will break through the frost-encrusted ground of adversity overnight.

The Law of History

No life is unhistorical or beyond history—no religious life and no secular life.[4] History is the means of man's existence. Development and growth: these shape the sphere of our existence, whether guided by the streams of interior mission or by self-willed decision. We may try to exist beyond history, outside of our actual situation, or to escape or react out of a false perspective, but these are temptations. Emigration and reaction do not belong to the categories of human life. "Hic Rhodus [Here is Rhodes]" applies and is a duty.[5] Anything else is escapism and calls a curse upon itself.

---

[3] Num 20:7–11: "The Lord spoke to Moses: . . . in the presence of the community, speak to the rock; it will let its water gush forth accordingly. . . . Moses raised his staff and struck the rock twice, and much water came forth." —TRANS.

[4] A theme from Fr. Delp's philosophical writings (ADGS 2). —TRANS.

[5] Fr. Delp refers to the famous sentence *Hic Rhodus, hic salta* ("The Braggart", an Aesop's Fable). [Aesop's fable tells of a man who boasted of having

The Gospel of the Fourth Sunday of Advent (Lk 3:1–6) reports history. It enumerates the power brokers who determined the structure of the small sphere where the light was about to appear and salvation would be proclaimed.

You have to remember the historical context of these names in order to know that a hopeless moment in history is signaled here. It was hopeless from Caesar's throne all the way down to the guards of the temple sanctuary. The visible priesthood was corrupt and entrenched in power politics, nepotism, and a hidebound clericalism.

Hopeless: that is the fetter history so often uses to bind salvation's hands. It discourages the hearts of those who know and sense what is happening, bringing them to trembling and despair, to cheap silence and weary resignation.

Our bondage through history, and to history, is something man needs to know, and Christians need to know. Trying to live outside history is lifelessness and a shadow existence. History is not the ultimate thing, but the Ultimate can be seen only in the context of history. Otherwise, life revolves around an idol that deceives; an idol with which we deceive ourselves and seek cheap consolation.

The Law of the Mysteries

In Goethe's opinion, "If it's into the infinite you wish to stride, go into the finite on every side."[6] The old man from Weimar proclaimed some great truths, but with respect to their metaphysical background, he was not very original. He

---

made an outstanding jump in Rhodes, only to be told, "Here is Rhodes, jump here!" What "applies and is a duty", according to Fr. Delp, is that we prove ourselves in the here and now. —TRANS.]

[6] *Goethes Werke*, vol. 1, 3rd ed. (Berlin: Christian Wegner Verlag, 1956), p. 304.

translated Spinoza's pantheistic thoughts into lyrics and into ostensible experiences. And yet, despite all his freedom and joy in experiencing the world, there is almost no more systematic and pessimistic dogmatist than Goethe regarding the deepest attitudes and assessments. The tension with Schiller, for example, was really nothing other than the inability to reconcile Kant with Spinoza.

That is just an aside. "Into the finite on every side" unveils nothing human. Rather, it reveals either the bond to an a priori assumption; or the recognition, the experience of a limit, of something veiled, of something ineffable and silent: the mystery.

It is precisely this "entering into the finite all around us", a universal grasp with which some great minds are gifted, that wakes man up to the consciousness of journeying through mysteries, being surrounded by them, and interiorly filled with them. In the end, the questions remain and the answers are lacking. The symbols remain and the interpretations are lacking. The events remain and the explanations for them are lacking.

Man makes every effort to pull this thorn out of the body of a smooth, comfortable existence. He overlooks exterior signs of reality, and dulls his senses with daily routine until the avalanche of life drives him out of the cozy homes and well-tended gardens into the streets of distress and wandering. Or else he keeps thinking up new categories he wants to impose upon reality: categories of reason, emotion, sense, or nonsense. He attempts this with skepticism, or with heroic pessimism, with *progressus infinitus*, or with Faustian ambition. Finally, he must either resign himself or invent a new category to distract him for a brief moment from the seriousness of his situation and the relentlessness of the unresolved questions.

Life happens within a greater context than man can cope with or understand. Life brings greater burdens and bears a richer cargo than we can cope with, comprehend, or manage alone. Everything that man would like to regard and attain to as the final end unveils itself as a preliminary, a new sign of the message, a new word of the message, a new question, a new assignment. In spite of being alert and willing, from an earthly perspective and earthly strength, life ultimately remains veiled, silent, taciturn, a *mystery*. It is secret and mysterious and, as such, uncanny.

The Threefold Law of Freedom

Man becomes truly himself only when he rises above himself. Only beyond himself do the power and strength exist, which he needs to be himself and to attain freedom—that freedom he needs as much as air and light for self-realization. Yet the fact remains that this power and strength become available and effective only through certain decisions—decisions made by and within the individual.

Overcoming the Law of Guilt

The liberating victory over the law of guilt is not to be found in the human heart just by calling for it. Insight and transformation of heart are preconditions man must fulfill in order to call upon and to encounter the supernatural, redeeming power that lies beyond himself. Nor does Advent call the converted heart to liberation in that way. "Excita potentiam tuam, per auxilium gratiæ tua [Awaken Your power; accompany us with Your grace]."[7] It is God Himself who stands in

---

[7] Liturgy for Fourth Sunday of Advent, Collect.

opposition to our guilt. Guilt is like fetters, which can be released only by the one who holds the key. And that person does not have the strong yearning that my heart has. Guilt is like my cell door. The key would not help me, even if I had one. There is no inside keyhole. The door can be opened only from the outside.

God stands in opposition to our guilt. He stands as Accuser and Judge when we persist in sin. He stands as Liberator and Savior when we turn to Him, uniting with Him against our sin. This means that the time of the great intercessors has come. They will lift up our need and our night to God and, at the same time, through the disposition and vigor of their hearts, they will bring our times into a deep union with God. The great outcry to God must begin and not let up. We must take Him at His word. After all, He wrote the law of prayer Himself. Compare Matthew 21:18ff., Luke 17:5, Luke 11:5ff., and many other Scripture passages that apply to the survival of the world. There is a confidence that calls out to Him, a confidence from which He likes to be called upon. The realization of many great things, of many genuine miracles, depends only upon our trust in God's great generosity. He will not always do a show-stopping miracle, although the show of power will sometimes be there. But He can and will, with divine sovereignty, so dispose the thousand small things of inner-world causality and logic, that in the end His will is accomplished. Anyone possessed of this confidence would be certain of the results; he would leave the means up to the Lord God. And anyone whose own self-reliance is overcome by the Lord in this way is left standing speechless and astonished.

The time of the great intercessors has come. Prayer does not mean some Quietist approach dispensing us from action and responsibility. To the contrary, this is a much harder principle of action. The time of pure action, simultaneously consecrated from within, has come. The precept of Ignatius, "*interiora sunt . . .*",[8] says that the interior life must fill and support the exterior efforts and make them fruitful. That is the precept for this time. Today more than ever, action, commitment, and achievement must unfold from devoted worship.

There is no reason to lose heart or give up and be depressed. Instead this is a time for confidence and for tirelessly calling on God. We must unite ourselves with God against our distress. Take these words seriously: "Fiat misericordia tua super nos, quæmadmodum speravimus in te [Let your mercy be upon us who have placed our hope in you]."[9] That establishes the measure to which God commits Himself. His nearness is as intimate as our longing is genuine. His mercy is as great as our call to Him is earnest. His liberation is as near and effective as our faith in Him and in His coming is unshaken and unshakable. That's the truth!

---

[8] *Summarium Constitutionum*, no. 16 (part X, no. 2). ["For the preservation and growth not only of the body or exterior of the Society but also of its spirit, and for the attainment of the objective it seeks, which is to aid souls to reach their ultimate and supernatural end, the means which unite the human instrument with God and so dispose it that it may be wielded well by His divine hand are more effective than those which equip it in relation to human beings. . . . Thus it appears that care should be taken in general that all the members of the Society devote themselves to the solid and perfect virtues and to spiritual pursuits, and attach greater importance to them than to learning and other natural and human gifts. *For these interior gifts are necessary to make those exterior means efficacious for the end which is being sought.*" In *The Constitutions of the Society of Jesus and Their Complementary Norms*, ed. John W. Padberg, S.J. (St. Louis, Mo.: Institute of Jesuit Sources, 1996), p. 400 (emphasis added). —TRANS.]

[9] From the hymn of praise: *Te Deum*.

Liberation from the Law of History

Beyond history, there is only One who is real and capable of all life: the pure Spirit, the Almighty God, the Lord of all history. Running away from history is not the great liberation. Liberation is, rather, the covenant with God within history, for the fulfillment of history.

You have to reread the Gospel in order to experience this. While this group and that group represented the law of history, while history was so hopeless and unspiritual all the way into the sanctuary of the Lord, then the Word of the Lord came to John.

And the result? The voice rings out, the people are set in motion, and the waters of the Jordan become a bath of liberation. The great breakthrough is proclaimed, and life is granted a tremendous promise. The narrowness falls away, and windows are forced open to reveal the view into the distance. In other words, it worked.

In history, testing includes both the departure, the journey into the desert to solitude and separation, and the return to the narrow streets of life. But the desert is not a place of refuge or a value in itself. Instead, it is a place of preparation, of waiting, of readiness, of listening for the word of commission.

These have been the laws of testing in history. Testing begins with a preparation for the mission, listening and being awake to the word, confidence and courageous confession of faith. And all this happens in one particular, historical moment; not at some moment one might wish for or imagine. This is where the law of devoted worship, audibly and visibly unfolding within history, is applied. That is what it is about.

And where this law is invoked upon history, history

comes under judgment and is called back to the duty of all creatures, the praise of the Lord. Here, as prison and fetters, history is overcome. For the Word of God is not fettered,[10] not even when all human values lie in the chains of anxiety, and fear, and despondency, and weariness, and habitual compromise.

Prepare the way. This is a call to enter into history. Again and again, history will yield herself to those loyal to this call, because she senses the presence of the Lord with this call and naturally tends toward lasting union with her true Source.

Overcoming the Law of the Mysteries

The message of the Fourth Sunday of Advent releases even this torturous fetter, in three ways. It impels us to recognition. Such is our life: "dispensatores mysteriorum—administrators of the mysteries" (1 Cor 4:1). It is a trial, to know about the mysteries, to bear the mysteries. This is a part of genuine worship, to know that *Deus semper maior* [God is always greater]. We must take this seriously, even when it starts with the hardship and incomprehensibility of anxious everyday life.

The news proclaims the consecration, proclaims that things are consecrated and, through God's nearness and God's intimacy of existence, the special mysteries are present among us. It fills time and circumstances with the blessedness of divine cargo. That is both merciful reality and, simultaneously, a special symbol of the whole. *Dispensatores*: as administrators of the mysteries, we must endure and speak out. This refers to mission again. Once we accept the night, light

---

[10] "That is my gospel, for which I bear every suffering, even wearing fetters like a criminal. But the Word of God is not fettered" (2 Tim 2:9). —TRANS.

will come. Once we accept history, it will hear the news of the Redeemer.

"Quoadusque veniat . . ." [Do not judge . . . before He comes . . .] (1 Cor 4:5). All of this is waiting and keeping watch for the coming of the Lord. "Dominus est" [It is the Lord who judges] (1 Cor 4:4). We must know the intimacy of God, the certainty of God within life. This great virtue of tirelessness[11] is called for here: the tirelessness, which is touched by the Lord and, with the strength from His touch, keeps rubbing the sleep from its eyes and stays awake. *Quoadusque*: keep journeying and keep awake. This is the law of the successful and liberated life.

God's are the day and the night, the fetters and the freedom, the prison and the wide world. In each of these, the deep sense of an encounter with God should fulfill itself. Only, one must demand the ultimate meaning of everything, ask every question down to the last. Our questions unveil themselves as questions seeking God and, at the same time, questions posed by God. Proclaim every answer down to the last. They unveil themselves as the message and annunciation of God. Endure every night until its middle.[12] It unveils itself as Christ-Mass, the Consecration-Night of God's arrival.[13] The knowers, the watchers, and the callers—those who

[11] In various prison letters, Fr. Delp mentioned "tirelessness" (*Unermüdlichkeit*) in the Pauline context of not growing weary. He called it "the virtue for our times", and wrote: "Tirelessness is truly a virtue, not just temperament." —TRANS.

[12] The Introit for the Sunday after Christmas reads: "As the universe was sunk in silence and the night had reached the middle of its course, Your almighty Word, O Lord, came down from Your royal throne of Heaven" (Wis 18:14). —TRANS.

[13] A wordplay in German: "*enthüllt sich als Weihe-Nacht*" means "unveils itself as Consecration-Night". Fr. Delp superimposed the root meaning of the German word for Christmas (*Weihnacht*) by writing: "*Weihe-Nacht*" (Consecration-Night). —TRANS.

know about God and His order, those who are awake and watching for Him, and those who are tirelessly calling Him— they will transform the fetters into a sacrament of freedom.

The Christmas Vigil

I wish you
Christmas of the heart
and of the spirit. . . .
May the Lord of the Holy Night,
the Lord of all days and nights,
give you His gracious protection.

— Alfred Delp, S.J.
  Letter to "Friends of Saint Blasien", December 1943
  (ADGS 5:166)

Liturgy for the Vigil Mass of the Nativity (December 24)

Introit: Exodus 16:6–7, Psalm 24(23):1

Hodie scietis, quia veniet Dominus, et salvabit nos: et mane videbitis gloriam ejus. Domini est terra, et plenitudo ejus: orbis terrarum, et universi, qui habitant in eo. Gloria Patri, et Filio, et Spiritui Sancto. Sicut erat in principio, et nunc, et semper, et in sæcula sæculorum. Amen.

Today you shall know that the Lord is coming to redeem us; and in the morning you shall see His glory. The earth and all its fullness belong to the Lord, the world and all who dwell therein. Glory be to the Father, and to the Son, and to the Holy Spirit. As it was in the beginning, is now, and ever shall be, world without end. Amen.

Collect:

Deus, qui nos redemptionis nostræ annua exspectatione lætificas: præsta; ut Unigenitum tuum, quem Redemptorem læti suscipimus, venientem quoque judicem securi videamus, Dominum nostrum Jesum Christum, Filium tuum. Qui tecum vivit et regnat in unitate Spiritus Sancti, Deus, per omnia sæcula sæculorum. Amen.

O God, every year we rejoice in the expectation of our Redemption; may we who joyfully receive Your only-begotten Son as our Savior also look with confidence upon Him when He comes as our judge, our Lord Jesus Christ, Your Son, who lives and reigns with You in the unity of the Holy Spirit, God, for ever and ever. Amen.

Epistle: Romans 1:1–6

Paulus, servus Jesu Christi, vocatus Apostolus, segregatus in Evangelium Dei, quod ante promiserat per Prophetas suos in Scripturis sanctis de Filio suo, qui factus est ei ex semine David secundum carnem: qui prædestinatus est Filius Dei in virtute secundum spiritum sanctificationis ex resurrectione mortuorum Jesu Christi Domine nostri: per quem accepimus gratiam, et apostolatum ad obediendum fidei in omnibus gentibus pro nomine ejus, in quibus estis et vos vocati Jesu Christi Domini nostri.

Paul, servant of Jesus Christ, called to be an apostle, set apart for the Gospel of God, in which, through His prophets in the Holy Scriptures, He gave promises beforehand about His Son, who is born of the line of David, according to the flesh. According to the Holy Spirit, He was predestined as the Son of God and proved Himself as such through His Resurrection from the dead, Jesus Christ our Lord. Through Him we have received the grace and our apostolic mission to bring all peoples to obedience in faith for the glory of His name. To such you also belong, among those called by Jesus Christ our Lord.

Gradual: Exodus 16:6–7, Psalm 80(79):2–3

Hodie scietis, quia veniet Dominus, et salvabit nos: et mane videbitis gloriam ejus.
V. Qui regis Israël, intende: qui deducis, velut ovem, Joseph: qui sedes super Cherubim appare coram Ephraim, Benjamin et Manasse.

Today you shall know that the Lord comes to redeem us; and in the morning you shall see His glory.

V. Attend, you shepherds of Israel, you who lead Joseph like a sheep. You who are enthroned above the cherubim, come and appear to Ephraim, Benjamin, and Manasseh.

Alleluia:

Alleluia, alleluia. Crastina die delebitur iniquitas terræ: et regnabit super nos Salvator mundi. Alleluia.

Alleluia, alleluia. Tomorrow the iniquity of the earth shall be abolished and the Savior of the world shall reign over us. Alleluia.

Gospel: Matthew 1:18–21

Cum esset desponsata mater Jesu Maria Joseph, antequam convenirent, inventa est in utero habens de Spiritu Sancto. Joseph autem vir ejus, cum esset justus, et nollet eam traducere, voluit occulte dimittere eam. Hæc autem eo cogitante, ecce, Angelus Domini apparuit in somnis ei, dicens: Joseph, filli David, noli timere accipere Mariam conjugem tuam: quod enim in ea natum est, de Spiritu Sancto est. Pariet autem filium, et vocabis nomen ejus Jesum: ipse enim salvum faciet populum suum a peccatis eorum.

At the time when Mary, the mother of Jesus, was betrothed to Joseph, before they had come together, it happened that she had conceived from the Holy Spirit. Because Joseph, her husband, was a just man and did not want to expose her publicly, he planned to separate from her secretly. While he was considering this, however, an angel of the Lord appeared to him in a dream and said, "Joseph, son of David, do not be afraid to take Mary for your wife, for what is conceived in her is of the Holy Spirit. She will give birth to a son. You shall give Him the name Jesus, for He will redeem His people from their sins."

Offertory: Psalm 24(23):7

Tollite portas, principes, vestras: et elevamini, portæ æternales, et introibit Rex gloriæ.

Open higher, O gates, open wide, eternal portals, and the King of glory will come in.

Secret:

Da nobis, quæsumus, omnipotens Deus: ut, sicut adoranda Fillii tui natalitia prævenimus, sic ejus munera capiamus sempiterna gaudentes: Qui tecum vivit et regnat in unitate Spiritus Sancti, Deus, per omnia sæcula sæculorum. Amen.

Grant, we beseech You, Almighty God, that through our vigil celebration of the birth of Your beloved Son we may joyously attain to His eternal benefits, who lives and reigns with You in the unity of the Holy Spirit, God, for ever and ever. Amen.

Communion: Isaiah 40:5

Revelabitur gloria Domini: et videbit omnis caro salutare Dei nostri.

The glory of the Lord will be revealed: and all flesh shall see the salvation of our God.

Postcommunion:

Da nobis, quæsumus, Domine: unigeniti Filii tui recensita nativitate respirare: cujus cælisti mysterio pascimur et potamur. Per eumdem Jesum Christum, Dominum nostrum, qui tecum vivit et regnat in unitate Spiritus Sancti, Deus, per omnia sæcula sæculorum. Amen.

Give us breath, we beseech You, O Lord, through the celebration of the birth of Your only-begotten Son whose heavenly mystery is our food and drink. Through the same Jesus Christ, our Lord, who lives and reigns with You in the unity of the Holy Spirit, God, for ever and ever. Amen.

Meditation for the Christmas Vigil
Written in Tegel Prison, Berlin
December 1944

The Blessed Burden of God

Christmas has always been subject to many misunderstandings. Superficialities, taking refuge in familiarity, idyllic playing around with Nativity scenes, and so forth, have displaced our view from the tremendous event this holy day represents.

This year the temptations toward a picturesque Christmas are probably reduced. The harshness and coldness of life have hit us with a previously unimaginable force. Some of us, whose homes cannot even offer the cold shelter of the stable in Bethlehem anymore, perhaps begin to forget the picturesque little ox and little donkey and to approach the question of what Christmas is really all about. Is the world more beautiful and life healthier because of that first Christmas? Because the angels finally and publicly sang their Gloria? Because the shepherds, awestruck, ran and adored? Because King Herod panicked and murdered the children? Well, here, the question is basically already obsolete. After all, that cruelty and those murders happened only because it was Christmas.

Yet, indeed, we will seldom pray a word so earnestly, honestly, and longingly as this *respirare* asking for breath at the close of the Christmas Eve Vigil Mass: Lord, give us breath.[1] Let us draw a deep breath because the stones have fallen from our hearts; because life is on solid ground again; because our perspective is free again; because the decision applies again; because the relative safety life normally affords is no longer devoured by the uncertainty that was inflated far beyond the norm.

Respirare! To be completely honest, I would like very much to do that soon myself. In yesterday's Mass, how wholeheartedly I prayed the words: "citius liberentur [speedily liberated]".[2] Every morning I have to mobilize myself for the day, and every evening I have to mobilize myself for the night. In between, I very often kneel or sit before my silent tabernacle and talk over my whole situation with Him. Without this continual contact with Him, I would have lost the ability to cope with the case and the situation long ago.

Well, here I can ask myself, personally and concretely, the same question that generally, and just as concretely, applies to Christmas. What is different, now that the Sacrament is in this narrow cell; now that the Mass is celebrated; now that someone prays and weeps; now that God is known and believed and called upon here? What is different because of it?

---

[1] Reference to the Postcommunion Prayer in the Christmas Vigil liturgy: "*Da nobis, quæsumus, Domine . . . respirare*—Give us breath, we beseech You, O Lord." See also "Meditation for the Third Sunday of Advent, 1944", p. 108. —TRANS.

[2] *Citius liberentur* refers to the Collect for the Mass on Ember Friday: "*Excita, quæsumus, Domine, potentiam tuam, et veni: ut hi, qui in tua pietate confidunt, ab omni citius adversitate liberentur: Qui vivis et regnas cum Deo Patre in unitate Spiritus Sancti, Deus, per omnia sæcula sæculorum. Amen.* [Awaken, O Lord, Your power and come, in order that those who trust in Your goodness may be speedily liberated from every adversity. You who live and reign with God the Father in the unity of the Holy Spirit, God, for ever and ever. Amen.]"

The reference to "yesterday" would be to Ember Friday, December 22, and indicates that Fr. Delp wrote these lines on Saturday, December 23, 1944. —TRANS.

At given times keys screech in the lock and hands are imprisoned in irons, and at given times released, and so it goes for us, the same day after day. What has all this to do with the "*respirare*" that the mystery of God brings about? What about that sitting and waiting for salvation? . . . For how long? And to what end?

One must take care to celebrate Christmas with a great realism. Otherwise, the emotions expect transformations the intellect cannot substantiate. Then the outcome of this most comforting of all holidays can be bitter disappointment and paralyzing weariness, especially these days.

The Christmas Eve Vigil Mass instructs us in a threefold temperance of expectation and realistic reflection.

The God Whose Coming We Celebrate
Remains the God of the Promise

In the Introit we pray: "Hodie scietis . . . mane videbitis . . . [Today you shall know . . . in the morning you shall see . . .]." This means, first, quite simply the nearness of the holy day, the relationship between the Vigil Mass and Christmas Day. However, it also means a continuing condition, a basic principle of our lives. Actually, one of the supporting and simultaneously torturous tensions of our existence is that man knows and has heard a great deal, and yet finds no resting place. Man wants so much to regard the known as if it were the final answer, and to feel at home there and settle himself firmly. Yet a supposition, an often quite uncomfortable presentiment, keeps coming to mind that this is not yet the end of the journey. Again and again, the reality—what one just had, and comprehended, and apprehended—reveals itself over time to be a sign of a greater reality, calling through the sign. Man must keep going, keep traveling toward life's prize.

To stop too soon would mean death, together with metaphysical and religious ruin.

This *mane videbitis* [in the morning you shall see] evokes a creative and healing restlessness in us, to which we are indebted for everything that is authentic and fully alive. But at what a price! Our Lord calls this condition "hunger and thirst after righteousness" [Mt 5:6]. Oh, you need to have counted the hours until your next piece of bread in order to know what this means, and what tension is involved in rising above and beyond the human condition.

Release of the tension (whether through avoidance, indifference, resignation, insensitivity, physical atrophy, destruction of the metaphysical nerves, overexertion, or weariness with life) is one of the deadly wounds from which modern man is bleeding to death. Eliminating the tension that strained one to the last nerve may have seemed like a relief at first, like liberation from an uncomfortable burden. Yet over time, one cannot avoid recognizing that these burdens are among the fixed conditions and prerequisites of life.

And now, at the gates of the Christmas mystery, through which we want to enter as though it were the rediscovered Paradise, the same motif will come into play: *Scietis—you will know* . . . You have heard and understood the message. *Videbitis—you shall see* . . . You should set out toward the tangible fulfillment and encounter. Here, too, is the old tension. Here, too, is the principle of archery: the bow can be drawn only when the archer bears the burden.

One should bear in mind that we are celebrating the feast of God becoming man, not yet the feast of man's relative divinization. The latter is starting, but in the human sphere and in world events. As the Epistle so stubbornly intones, "ex semine David secundum carnum . . . [of the line of David according to the flesh . . .]" (Rom 1:1–6). That is how man must understand it. It is the incomprehensible fact of God entering into history;[3] that He stepped into our law, into our space, into our existence—and not only like one of us, but as one of us. That is the thrill and the incomprehensibility of this event.

History now becomes the Son's mode of existence; historical destiny becomes His destiny. He is to be encountered on our streets. In the darkest cellars and the loneliest prisons of life, we will meet Him. And that is already the first blessing and consecration of the burden: that He is to be met under its weight.

Along with the first blessing, there is a second: All those hauling the same load feel it when a new, powerful shoulder places itself under the burden and joins in the carrying.

And let the third blessing be spoken simultaneously with the other two: ever since that Holy Night, the divine-human life became the primordial model of existence, according to which all life will be formed by God, if we do not resist this formation. The strength for mastery of life grows through the influx of divine life among those to whom Christ has made Himself known, among the greater human community as well as small groups brought together by circumstance.

We will be better able to cope with life, more efficient and capable of life, if we open ourselves to the instructions of this coming night. Let us hike and journey onward, neither avoiding nor shunning the streets and terror of life. Something new has been born in us, and we do not want to tire of believing the star of the promises and acknowledging the singing angels' *Gloria*—even if it is sometimes through tears. Our distress has truly become transformed, because we have been raised above it.

[3] The German, "*der Eingeschichtlichung Gottes*", is unusual and has the sense of "*historicization* of God". —TRANS.

The God of the Christmas Encounter
Remains the God of Challenge

The Christmas-time image of God has been exposed to the most misunderstandings. Man remains attached to the appearance and so often feels absolutely nothing of the overwhelming thrill and basically terrifying incomprehensibility that touches us through this birth of God as a human child. To be sure, all the imagery has been a great comfort to generations of people, as well as to the individual. Moreover, since then, man has had more right to approach the throne of God with confidence and to plead with Him. God is on our side.

This does not mean, however, that God has abdicated His role as God, anymore than the foregoing meant that man's fate would become a smiling meadow or a bed of roses. Observe the obliteration of the divine features from the face of the Child, and later, of the man, Jesus; first diffusing and softening it into the idyllic, Christmas-cheery image of children's stories; later, reducing Christ Himself into an upstanding citizen who offered a good example and pious admonitions. These are very serious contributing causes of the powerlessness that has thrown the Western world's concept of God into chains.

It was, and it still is, *God* who became man. Unlike us, God—even as man—remains the Lord of all creatures and of all creation. In His presence, in reverence and adoration, man must wake up to himself, because only then can he let go of himself and arrive at the ultimate reality. Only there are we whole.

The Vigil Mass twice proclaims this circumspection with which we should enter into the sanctuary of this feast. First, in the Epistle, Paul says of his relationship to Christ: "Ad obediendum fidei in omnibus gentibus [Through Him we received grace and our apostolic mission to bring all peoples to obedience in faith]" (Rom 1:5). Leaving aside the Pauline excess, the precept is obvious here. All encounters with God challenge His creatures to response and mission. Whoever is drawn into the breath of God is also drawn into the law of His life. Further, for His creatures, this means that the nearer we are to God, the more we are bound to both this current and nature's yearning for home.

God's nearness is a searching nearness, and whoever has come to know this nearness will be simultaneously swept up into that tirelessness with which God presses near to mankind.[4] Experiencing God's merciful restlessness toward mankind reveals how much one has understood of the mysterious relationship between God and man. In that relationship, there is no *sacro egoismo*.[5] Instead, the natural law of the streets becomes transformed into the destiny of mission.

A second time, the liturgy rescues the image of the incarnate God from the danger of being seen as delicate and innocuous. The liturgy draws our attention to another untouched fundamental relationship between God and creature. In the Collect, suddenly and unexpectedly, we are reminded that the Child at whose coming we are rejoicing is the future Judge of our lives.

These smiling eyes of the Child will someday focus on us in mature, solemn examination and judgment. Even after Christmas, and as a consequence of our growing capacity for

[4] In the "Meditation for the Fourth Sunday of Advent, 1944" (see p. 151), Fr. Delp used the word "tirelessness" in reference to man's tirelessness in seeking and serving God. Here, he presents its counterpart: God's tirelessness in seeking us. —TRANS.

[5] In 1915, Italy's prime minister Antonio Salandro coined the expression "sacro egoismo" (sacred egoism or self-interest) to justify Italy's entrance into World War I on the side of the Allies. —TRANS.

a successful life gained from these mysteries, man continues to be tested and called to account.

Oh, the Child is really already judging the world now! How many types of people today honestly could appear at the manger? Most of them have absolutely no desire to do so. The small, scanty door does not let anyone riding a high horse get through. The simple, wholesome shepherds find the way. The royal wise men are called by the star. But the usurper of Jerusalem feared the Child. How much of what we are living through today cannot stand in the presence of the Child! How would our own lives, and life in general, be different if we remembered that life's greatest hour was when God became man, a child? We would not approach one another, stand before one another so demandingly, and violently, and greedily. Children do not inflict such wounds. We want to be so great and mighty, so grown up and competent. We ourselves, and the heap of rubble that is left to us, are the outcome of this attitude.

From Child to Crucified, every hour of His life that healed and liberated us is a judgment over the way we live. That is why we are so beaten, bound, and in distress. And that also is why His ultimate hour is the Resurrection, the victorious return home. Our lives, however, are so hopelessly beset. We ought to take the Child very seriously.

The God over Whose Coming We Rejoice
Remains the God of Trials

That these principles of promise and challenge apply is, in itself, already enough of a trial. And that the Lord requires our obedience to the message, our unshakable accordance to the word upon which we must base our lives, only emphasizes this burden. Yet that is still not the end. These are just

general principles and regulations of life, and above and beyond all these, something else is there. It is the personal
providence and guidance through which God intervenes in
our individual lives—and so often He seems to leave us alone
with the burden He has laid upon us.

You have to read the Gospel of the Vigil (Mt 1:18–21)
from a personal perspective. I mean, understand it as a report
about Mary's life. Of course, we already know the outcome,
the resolution, and redemption. Yet what a time she had to
go through! Joseph's faith in regard to a person was put to the
test, but think of Mary!

She had really given herself to God. Her Yes held nothing
back and was unconditional. The Word of the Lord came to
her in an eminent way, as it will never again come to any
creature. And then God was silent. She felt Joseph's questioning eyes. She sympathized with the torture of his faithful
heart, the suffering and disappointment of the righteous
man. Moreover, at first God left her alone during that time,
beneath that burden. Think it through, from a personal
perspective.

Again and again, that is our destiny. We have heard promises and believed messages and felt we had a mission. Then
suddenly we are left hanging alone with our fate. That is how
it goes in human life. Even in Christian life? Especially for us,
should it not be very different and our expectations fully
apply? But that's the way it is.

These are precisely the decisive moments for proving what
our faith life is worth. Despite the evidence of the stone
against which we strike our foot, despite the evidence of the
scourge that beats us bloody, despite the evidence of the
chains that bind us, we must abide in the Word, unshaken and
tireless—remain standing. That is the great answer that man
can give to God, and God will ask each one of us about it.

Each one. No one will be spared the test if he is to be counted as awake and mature in the presence of God the Lord.

God poses these questions today by the hundred. May we be capable of answering! Practicing the virtue of tirelessness is strenuous, but that is what makes us capable of God and opens our eyes to the actual reality of God.

Where man seriously attempts this, the face of the earth is renewed. The hard features of inner world causality, logical connections, and necessity soften. The face of the world and of life becomes more motherly, and more fatherly. The mystery of the hundreds and hundreds of little gifts God showers upon us begins. Things and connections remain in their course and tendency, yet within them, within their quiet assent to a new order, God bestows a new experience of His fatherly concern on those who were up to His questions. All at once, man learns that the world's course is no longer so universal with its generally applicable principles, but that things have a greater meaning and value. At the pinnacle of human existence—personal dialogue between God and man—experiences have a completely different value than do ordinary events. And it is only right that an event which to one person appears mere banal daily routine is for someone else a sign of mercy and guidance.

Respirare

And here we have arrived at the heights upon which the *respirare*—the sigh of relief, the new breath—can happen and may happen and should happen. The world continues on its course, but it has become the barque of the Lord God that no storm can overturn and no flood can tear asunder. The same principles and tensions of life continue to apply, but the Lord God has subjected Himself to these tensions and entered into them. He bears them with us, thereby increasing the potential for strength and independence of all of mankind.

Lastly, man is no longer alone. The monologue was never a healthy or satisfying way of life. Man's life is authentic and healthy only in dialogue. All these "mono-tendencies" are from evil. Yet, because enduring the tensions of existence and the burdens from God calls man into dialogue with Him, it conquers the most terrible human ailment, loneliness, finally and truly. Now there is no more night without light, no prison cell without genuine conversation, no solitary mountain path or dangerous ravine without accompaniment and guidance.

God is with us: that was the promise, and we have wept and pleaded for it. And it has been realized in accordance with each individual's capacity, and each life's capacity: completely different, much more fulfilled, and, at the same time, much simpler than we thought.

We should not avoid the burdens God gives us. They lead us into the blessing of God. To those who remain faithful to the ascetic and hard life, the interior springs of reality will be unsealed, and the world is not silent as we might have thought. The silver threads of God's mysteries within everything that is real begin sparkling and singing. The burden is blessed, because it has been recognized and carried as a burden from God.

God becomes man. Man does not become God. The human order remains and continues to be our duty, but it is consecrated. And man has become something more, something mightier. Let us trust life because this night must lead to light. Let us trust life because we do not have to live it alone. God lives it with us.

APPENDIX I

Chronology: 1907–1945

No life is unhistorical or beyond history. . . .
History is not the ultimate thing,
but the Ultimate can be seen
only in the context of history.

— Alfred Delp, S.J.
 Meditation for the Fourth Sunday of Advent, 1944

In the Chronology, references to Fr. Delp's Advent writings
appear in **bold** type.

CHRONOLOGY

ALFRED DELP'S LIFE	HISTORICAL EVENTS

ALFRED DELP'S LIFE

1907—SEPTEMBER 15: Born in Mannheim, Germany.

SEPTEMBER 17: Baptized at Catholic Church of SS. Ignatius of Loyola and Francis Xavier, Mannheim.

1913—Begins elementary schooling in Hüttenfeld.

1914—DECEMBER: His family moves to Lampertheim; his father is drafted into German Army.

HISTORICAL EVENTS

1882—Germany, Austria-Hungary, and Italy form "Triple Alliance".

1907—Great Britain, France, and Russia unite in "Triple Entente". *German Reich*: Kaiser Wilhelm II *Austria-Hungary*: Franz Joseph I *Italy*: King Victor Emmanuel III *Great Britain*: King Edward VII *France*: Emile Combes leads coalition government. *Russia*: Czar Nicholas II

1910—MAY 6: Britain: Edward VII dies. Reign of King George V begins.

1912—NOVEMBER: U.S.: Woodrow Wilson is elected President.

1914—JUNE 28: Heir to the Austro-Hungarian throne, Franz Ferdinand, is assassinated in Serbia.

JULY 28: World War I begins.

AUGUST 3–4: Germany invades Belgium. Germany and Austria-Hungary ("Central Powers") oppose France, Russia, Britain ("Triple Entente"). Because Germany and Austria-Hungary are the aggressors, Italy does not support them. The U.S. remains neutral.

AUGUST 20: Vatican: Pope Pius X dies, is succeeded by Benedict XV.

OCTOBER: Turkey enters war on side of Central Powers.

1915—JANUARY: Enrolls in Lutheran elementary school according to his father's wishes, but attends Catholic Mass regularly with his mother and siblings.

1915—APRIL–MAY: Poison gas is used in battle for the first time: Ypres, Belgium.

MAY 7: German submarine sinks British passenger ship *Lusitania*.

MAY 24: Italy enters the war on the side of the Allies (France, Russia, and Britain).

1916—JULY–NOVEMBER: Battle of Verdun: more than 1 million soldiers die, with no important gain to either side.

NOVEMBER: U.S.: President Wilson is reelected.

1917—MARCH: Russia: Czar Nicholas II is forced to abdicate.

APRIL 6: U.S. enters the war on the side of the Allies.

MAY–OCTOBER: Portugal: apparitions of Our Lady at Fatima.

NOVEMBER 7–8: Russia: Lenin leads the "October Revolution", seizes power in the new Soviet Union.

DECEMBER: Central Powers win the eastern front; Soviet Union signs truce.

1918—JANUARY 8: President Wilson presents "Fourteen Points" peace plan.

JULY 16: Russia: Murder of Czar Nicholas II and his wife and children.

NOVEMBER 9: Germany: Kaiser Wilhelm II abdicates, flees to Holland, leaving Germany a political and economic shambles.

NOVEMBER 11: Armistice Day. WWI ends. More than 8.5 million soldiers are dead, and more than 21 million wounded.

1919—FEBRUARY 6: Germany: Friedrich Ebert (1871–1925) is elected President.

AUTUMN–WINTER: Germany: Hitler (1889–1945) joins right-wing German Workers' Party.

1920—NOVEMBER: His father is discharged from the army.

1920—JANUARY: Germany signs Treaty of Versailles.

NOVEMBER: U.S.: Warren G. Harding is elected President.

1921—MARCH 28: Receives Lutheran Confirmation.

APRIL–MAY: Makes personal decision to be a Catholic.

JUNE 19: Receives (Catholic) First Communion.

JUNE 28: Receives (Catholic) Confirmation.

1922—SPRING: Is enrolled in Catholic preparatory school in Dieburg as boarding student.

1922—JANUARY 22: Vatican: Pope Benedict XV dies, is succeeded by Pius XI.

OCTOBER 28: Italy: Mussolini seizes power.

1923—NOVEMBER 8–9: Hitler unsuccessfully attempts to seize power (Munich "Beer Hall" Putsch) and is sentenced to prison. German Workers' Party is banned. In prison, Hitler writes *Mein Kampf.*

1924—JANUARY: Is instrumental in founding a "New Germany" Catholic youth group at his school; becomes student leader of group.

1924—JANUARY: Russia: Lenin dies, is succeeded by Joseph Stalin.

NOVEMBER: U.S.: Calvin Coolidge is elected President.

DECEMBER: Hitler is released from prison and reestablishes German Workers' Party as National Socialist German Workers' Party (NSDAP or Nazi Party).

1925—FEBRUARY 28: Germany's
President, Friedrich Ebert, dies.
APRIL 26: General Paul von
Hindenburg (1847–1934) is elected
President of German Republic.

1926—MARCH 16: Graduates from
prep school at top of his class.
APRIL 22: Enters Society of Jesus
(Jesuit Order); begins novitiate at
Feldkirch.

1928—APRIL 27: Makes first vows.
AUTUMN: Begins philosophy studies in
Pullach.

1928—NOVEMBER: U.S.: Herbert
Hoover is elected President.

1929—JUNE: Pius XI introduces new
Mass for Feast of the Sacred Heart.
OCTOBER 23: New York Stock Market
crash: Great Depression begins in
U.S.; related economic crisis
worldwide, including Germany;
millions unemployed.

1931—APRIL 8–10: Receives tonsure,
minor orders.
JUNE: Takes final examination in
philosophy.
JULY: Is assigned to work at Jesuit
boarding school Stella Matutina in
Feldkirch as prefect.

1932—APRIL: Hitler runs for
president against Hindenburg, loses
with one-third of the vote.
NOVEMBER: U.S.: Franklin D.
Roosevelt is elected President.

1933—JANUARY 30: His first
publication, an article critical of
Martin Heidegger's *Being and Time*,
is published in *Aufstiege zur
Metaphysik Heute und ehedem*, ed. B.

1933—JANUARY 30: Hindenburg
names Hitler Chancellor of
Germany. Support for Nazi Party is
at 33.1%; Social Democrats, 20.4%;
Communist Party, 16.9%.

Jansen, S.J., Freiburg (French translation published 1935).

FEBRUARY 27: Reichstag fire: Parliament building is burned; Communists are accused of arson.

FEBRUARY 28: Emergency legislation limits civil rights, suspending freedom of the press, freedom to express opinions, and right to assemble. No right to privacy in communication by mail, telephone, or telegraph. Government search and seizure of private property is allowed. (Legislation, enacted as temporary emergency measure, becomes permanent.)

MARCH 3: Widespread arrests of Communists.

MARCH 5: Parliamentary election: Nazi Party receives 43.9% of vote; Social Democrats, 18.3%; Communists, 12.1%.

MARCH 21: Parliament passes the Enabling Act, giving Hitler full power to issue decrees and enact legislation independent of parliamentary approval.

MARCH 25: Walter Gempp (1878–1939), Berlin fire department director, is dismissed for publicizing evidence linking Nazis to Reichstag fire. (He is murdered in prison in 1939.)

APRIL 1: National Boycott Day: Nazi-ordered boycott of Jewish-owned businesses.

MAY 2: All German trade unions are absorbed into Nazi trade union, German Labor Front.

MAY 10: Books by Jewish and Communist authors are listed as prohibited and publicly burned.

MAY 27: Martin Heidegger gives pro-Nazi speech at University of Freiburg.

JUNE–JULY: Nazi Party becomes the only political party in Germany. All other parties are officially abolished.

JULY 11: Constitution is drawn up for the Lutheran churches in Germany, to define and protect religious rights of member churches under the new government.

JULY 20: Vatican signs concordat to protect religious rights of Catholics in Germany.

JULY 28: Law to "Prevent Hereditary Illness" is announced: forced sterilization of people with hereditary mental or physical disabilities is required after January 1, 1934.

SEPTEMBER 21: Pastor Martin Niemöller founds Pastors' Emergency League to preserve religious rights of Protestant churches in Germany.

SEPTEMBER 22: Reich Chamber of Culture is established to assess and assure state loyalty of artists and writers.

DECEMBER 21: Stella Matutina School: Delp's students perform *The Eternal Advent*, the Advent play he wrote for them.

OCTOBER 14: Germany withdraws from League of Nations.

1934—MARCH–APRIL: For political reasons, Stella Matutina is forced to relocate to St. Blasien.

1934—JANUARY: Law to "Prevent Hereditary Illness" takes effect: in its first year, there are 32,268 forced sterilizations.

FEBRUARY: Church youth groups are amalgamated into Hitler Youth.

FEBRUARY 7: Catholic Church places Alfred Rosenberg's racist book *The Myth of the Twentieth Century* on the index of books dangerous to morals.

APRIL 24: People's Court (*Volksgerichtshof*) is established and given total jurisdiction over cases of treason, with judges to be appointed by Hitler. Court decisions cannot be appealed.

MAY 29–31: "Barmen Declaration" defines the duties of Christians (loyalty to God has priority over loyalty to state), refutes the errors of pro-Nazi "German Christians", and unites the anti-Nazi Protestant groups into new "Confessing Church" movement.

JUNE 30: SS performs bloody 3-day purge, arresting or murdering Hitler's political enemies under the pretext of preventing a revolt.

AUGUST 2: Hindenburg dies. Hitler becomes President and Supreme Commander of the Armed Forces, in addition to his position as Chancellor, uniting all three high offices under one title: *Führer*, "Leader". All members of armed forces are immediately required to swear new oath of loyalty—not to Germany, but to the person of the Führer.

AUTUMN: Begins theology studies in Valkenburg, Holland.

NOVEMBER 19: Joseph Spieker, Jesuit priest in Cologne, Germany, is arrested for "misuse of the pulpit" (speaking against the government in a sermon or homily), a crime since March 21, 1933. He is the first Jesuit sent to a concentration camp.

1935—Publishes his first book, *Tragic Existence*, a criticism of Martin Heidegger's philosophy (Spanish translation published 1942). Contributes articles and book reviews to the homiletic periodical *Chrysologus*.

1935—MARCH 16: Hitler announces that German military service will be compulsory.

SEPTEMBER 15: Nuremberg Race Laws abolish civil rights of Jewish and "non-Aryan" citizens: voting and holding public office are forbidden them; "mixed" marriages are void and illegal, under penalty of imprisonment.

NOVEMBER 14: Reich Citizenship Amendment deprives Jews of German citizenship.

1936—Publishes *Advent 1935* in *Chrysologus*.
Begins publishing articles and book reviews in *Der Gral*, and in the Jesuit magazine *Stimmen der Zeit*.

1936—JANUARY 20: England: George V dies. Reign of King Edward VIII begins.
MARCH: Germany seizes demilitarized zone of Rhineland.
AUGUST: Olympic Games in Berlin: no nation publicly protests Nazi policies or boycotts the Games.
SEPTEMBER: Axis Treaty between Germany and Italy.

OCTOBER: Begins further theology studies in Frankfurt.

OCTOBER: Germany's treaty with Japan.
DECEMBER 1: Membership in Hitler Youth and in League of German Girls becomes mandatory for all Aryan youths.
DECEMBER 11: King Edward VIII abdicates British throne to marry Wallis Simpson. Succeeded by King George VI.

1937—MARCH 6–7: Is ordained as subdeacon and deacon in Frankfurt Cathedral.

1937—MARCH 14: Pope Pius XI issues *Mit brennender Sorge*, an encyclical criticizing Nazi violations of religious and human rights. Read from all Catholic pulpits on Passion Sunday. Nazis retaliate with arrests, closure of 12 printing firms.
APRIL–MAY: Munich Jesuit Rupert Mayer, outspoken opponent of Nazism, is banned from preaching or speaking publicly anywhere in the Reich.

JUNE 24: Is ordained to priesthood, at St. Michael Church, Munich, by Michael Cardinal von Faulhaber (400th jubilee of the ordination of St. Ignatius of Loyola).
JULY 4: Celebrates his first Holy Mass

JUNE 5: Rupert Mayer defies ban and is arrested for preaching in St. Michael Church, Munich.

JULY 1: Lutheran Pastor Martin

at hometown parish of St. Andreas, Lampertheim.

1938—JUNE 25: Recieves graduate degree in theology.

SEPTEMBER: Begins tertianship, the final year of Jesuit formation, focused on deepening the spiritual life.

1939—JULY 15: Receives Roman licentiate in theology and doctorate in philosophy.

JULY 25: His application to University of Munich for sociology studies is refused on political grounds. Begins work for Jesuit publication *Stimmen der Zeit*. Preaches regularly in Munich, and is offered speaking engagements throughout Germany.

Niemöller is arrested and imprisoned in concentration camps until end of the war.

1938—MARCH 12: Germany annexes Austria.
AUGUST 10: Hitler calls for war to reclaim Sudetenland territory. Colonel-General Ludwig Beck resigns in protest.
SEPTEMBER: Military officers and German Resistance secretly plan to arrest Hitler if Czechoslovakia is attacked.
OCTOBER 10: Munich agreement derails planned coup. British Prime Minister, Neville Chamberlain, negotiates peace at cost of Czechoslovakia. Hitler is given Sudetenland.
NOVEMBER 8–10: *Kristallnacht*: organized Nazi atrocities against Jewish communities throughout Germany.

1939—FEBRUARY 10: Death of Pope Pius XI.
MARCH 2: Cardinal Pacelli becomes Pope Pius XII.
SUMMER: Carl Goerdeler, Fabian Schlabrendorf, Adam von Trott zu Solz, and others opposed to Hitler share their concerns and seek support for Resistance in England and U.S.
AUGUST 23: Germany and Soviet Union sign nonaggression pact.
SEPTEMBER 1: Germany invades Poland.
SEPTEMBER 3: Britain and France declare war on Germany.
SEPTEMBER 17: Soviet Union invades Poland.

OCTOBER: Hitler orders euthanasia of people with disabilities, psychiatric patients, and chronically ill, categorized as "useless eaters", resulting in the murder of an estimated 100,000 Germans over a 2-year period.

OCTOBER: Vatican envoy Joseph Müller seeks to establish contact between British government and Vatican.

OCTOBER–FEBRUARY: Adam von Trott zu Solz visits U.S. on behalf of German Resistance movement, seeks Allied assistance.

NOVEMBER 8: Georg Elser (1903–1945) attempts to assassinate Hitler; is sentenced to Dachau Concentration Camp (murdered there on April 9, 1945).

DECEMBER 14: *Klostersturm*, Nazi seizure of monasteries and property belonging to Catholic religious orders, begins.

1940—Becomes active in Munich's *Una Sancta* group, local branch of the ecumenical movement founded by Fr. Max Joseph Metzger (1887–1944).

1940—APRIL: Germany invades Denmark and Norway.

MAY: Germany invades Holland, Belgium, Luxembourg, France. In Britain, Winston Churchill becomes Prime Minister.

JUNE 10: Italy enters war as ally of Germany.

JUNE 22: France signs armistice with Germany; Charles de Gaulle pledges continued French resistance.

JULY–OCTOBER: Battle of Britain: Germany begins mass air bombings of Britain.

1941—APRIL 18: His editorial work for *Stimmen der Zeit* ends as Gestapo seize its building.

1941—APRIL 18: Jesuit-owned *Stimmen der Zeit* building is seized by Gestapo in the course of *Klostersturm*.

JUNE 13: Reich Chamber of Culture refuses Fr. Delp's application to publish.

JUNE 16: He is assigned as rector of St. Georg Church, part of Heilig Blut Parish (under pastor Fr. Max Blumschein, assisted by Fr. Hermann Joseph Wehrle). Around this time Fr. Delp becomes active in helping Jewish and other political refugees to escape the country.

SEPTEMBER: Pupils from parish raise money to purchase new crosses; Fr. Delp blesses crucifixes for members of St. Georg Church taking part in the "Crucifix Action". Mothers and pupils replace all missing crosses in classrooms of nearby elementary and high schools.

OCTOBER: Fathers Delp and Paul Bolkovac, S.J., sign Herder publishing contract for collaborative work with Karl Rahner on dogmatic theology. Fr. Delp becomes seriously ill with abscessed teeth and middle-ear infection. Delp's illness and other work prevent the three from working together.

OCTOBER 22–23: Speaks at Men's Apostolate conference in Fulda.

NOVEMBER 30: *Homily for First Sunday of Advent.*

DECEMBER 5: Receives news from his sister Greta that her husband, Fritz Kern, was killed in action. Fr. Delp remains too ill to travel to Lampertheim.

JUNE 21: Germany invades Russia.

JULY–AUGUST: Clemens August von Galen, Catholic bishop of Münster, preaches against Germany's euthanasia program.

SEPTEMBER: In Bavaria, traditional crosses and crucifixes, removed from classrooms during summer vacation, are replaced by students; school administrators remove new crosses, suspend pupils who took part, warn their parents and report them to the Gestapo.

SEPTEMBER 1: All Jewish residents of Germany and occupied territories are required to wear yellow star.

OCTOBER 23: Cathedral Provost Bernhard Lichtenberg is arrested for his daily, public prayers for the Jews and all prisoners in concentration camps. As he is led to his cell in Plötzensee Prison, he loudly sings the "Salve Regina".

NOVEMBER 25: Eleventh Ruling on Reich Citizenship: all non-Aryan Germans are deprived of citizenship and given 3-week deadline to register for "emigration".

DECEMBER 7: *Homily for Second Sunday of Advent.*

DECEMBER 14: *Homily for Third Sunday of Advent.*

DECEMBER 21: *Homily for Fourth Sunday of Advent.*

DECEMBER 7: Japanese bomb Pearl Harbor.

DECEMBER 11: Hitler declares war on U.S.

1942—JANUARY–FEBRUARY: Fr. Delp is hospitalized for several weeks because of extracted teeth and severe infection.

MARCH: Has his first meeting with Count Helmuth James von Moltke.

1942—JANUARY 20: Wannsee Conference agrees on "Final Solution".

APRIL: Moltke and Dietrich Bonhoeffer travel to Norway to seek support for Resistance peace efforts.

MAY 22: Fr. Bernard Lichtenberg stands trial, gets 2-year prison sentence.

MAY 22–25: First Kreisau Conference at Moltke's estate (Pentecost weekend).

JULY 26: Holland's Catholic bishops protest German persecution of Jews with open pastoral letter to Reich Commissioner.

JULY 31–AUGUST 2: Meets in Berlin with Moltke, Trott zu Solz, and others to prepare for Kreisau Conference. Through Fr. Delp, Moltke is invited to meet with Bishops Preysing, Faulhaber, and Dietz.

AUGUST 22–23: Meets with Kreisau Circle in Berlin.

AUGUST 2: In Holland, mass arrests and deportations of Christian Jews, including Edith Stein and her sister, Rosa.

AUGUST 9: Edith Stein and companions are murdered in Auschwitz.

OCTOBER 16–18: Speaks at Kreisau Conference about Catholic social teaching.

OCTOBER 25: Moltke visits Fr. Delp in Munich.

OCTOBER 16–18: Second Kreisau Conference at Moltke's estate.

OCTOBER 31: Pius XII consecrates world to Immaculate Heart of Mary. [Vigil of All Saints.]

NOVEMBER 25: Visits Moltke in Berlin.

DECEMBER 4?: *Homily for Advent Holy Hour.*
DECEMBER 6: *Homily for Second Sunday of Advent.*
DECEMBER 13: *Homily for Third Sunday of Advent.*
DECEMBER 22: *Pre-Christmas Reflection.*

1943—Publishes *Man and History.*
JANUARY 20: Moltke visits Jesuit Provincial, Augustin Rösch, and Fr. Delp in Munich.

FEBRUARY 15: Unbeknownst to Fr. Delp, a parishioner, Maria Urban, writes a letter in which she offers her life to God as a sacrifice in the hope that Fr. Delp will survive his dangerous work for the Resistance movement.

NOVEMBER 22—FEBRUARY 2: Battle of Stalingrad: German Sixth Army is surrounded.

1943—JANUARY 14–24: Casablanca Conference—Roosevelt and Churchill agree Germany must surrender unconditionally.
FEBRUARY 2: Germany's 6th Army surrenders at Stalingrad.
FEBRUARY 18: Goebbels' speech in Berlin calls for "Total War". Munich's student opposition, the "White Rose" group, is arrested for anti-war leafleting and graffiti.
FEBRUARY 22: Hans and Sophie Scholl and Christopher Probst, of "White Rose", are tried in Munich by Judge Roland Freisler of the People's Court. They are convicted, sentenced to death, and executed the same day.
MARCH: Berlin's St. Hedwig Cathedral is in ruins after Allied bombing.
APRIL 5: Arrests of Hans von Dohnanyi and Dietrich and Klaus Bonhoeffer (key members of Defense Department Resistance).
APRIL 19: Second "White Rose" trial, again under Judge Roland Freisler. Professor Kurt Huber and students Willi Graf and Alexander Schmorell are condemned to death.

JUNE 12–14: Participates in the Kreisau Conference.

JUNE 12–14: Third Kreisau Conference at Moltke's estate.

JUNE 29: Fr. Max Joseph Metzger, founder of *Una Sancta* movement, is arrested for writing a letter to the Lutheran bishop of Sweden, proposing a peace program.

JULY 13: Professor Kurt Huber and Alexander Schmorell are executed in Munich.

OCTOBER 2–3: Bombing destroys many homes around St. Georg Church. Neighboring Heilig Blut Church burns to the ground.

OCTOBER 14: "White Rose" member Willi Graf is executed in Munich. Fr. Max Joseph Metzger, *Una Sancta* founder, convicted by Judge Roland Freisler and sentenced to death.

NOVEMBER 3: Fr. Bernard Lichtenberg, after serving his full prison sentence, remains in "protective custody", dies during transport to Dachau Concentration Camp. (Beatified 1996.)

NOVEMBER 28: *Homily for First Sunday of Advent.*

NOVEMBER 16: Thousands attend Fr. Lichtenberg's funeral.

1944—APRIL 24–25: Night of bombing damages roof, windows, and doors of St. Georg Church and rectory. Massive damage throughout Munich.

1944—JANUARY 19: Count Helmuth James von Moltke is arrested.

APRIL 17: Fr. Max Joseph Metzger is executed in Berlin. Beatification process opened May 2006.

JUNE 4: Bombing in Lampertheim damages Fr. Delp's parents' residence, forcing them to move.

JUNE 4: Allies liberate Rome.

JUNE 6: Visits Claus von Stauffenberg in Bamberg.

JUNE 6: D-Day: American and British forces land at Normandy.

JUNE 13: His neighbor and parishioner Maria Urban ("Urbi") is killed when a bomb destroys her house in a morning air raid.

JUNE 17: Fr. Delp receives from a friend Maria Urban's letter in which she had offered her life to God for his sake; deeply moved, he keeps

letter with him, even in prison.
[Feast of the Sacred Heart.]

JULY 20: Helps Paepcke family repair roof of their home in Pasing, a Munich suburb. At 6 P.M., while with Kreuser family in Bogenhausen, hears radio report of attempted coup. Later that night Fr. von Tattenbach warns him to go into hiding, but he refuses. He is scheduled to profess his final vows on August 15.

JULY 28: He is arrested after morning Mass at St. Georg.

AUGUST 6—7: He is transferred to Moabit Prison, Berlin. [Feast of the Transfiguration.]

AUGUST 14–15: Undergoes "intensive" interrogation (torture).

AUGUST 15: Marianne Hapig brings food and clean laundry to Fr. Delp for the first time. [Feast of the Assumption.]

SEPTEMBER 27: He is transferred to Tegel Prison.

OCTOBER 1: Begins secretly celebrating daily Mass.

OCTOBER 7: A bomb blast close to the prison knocks Fr. Delp unconscious. [First Friday.]

JULY 20: Claus Schenk von Stauffenberg attempts to assassinate Hitler. Co-conspirators stand by in Berlin, prepared to seize government. The attempted coup fails.

JULY 21: Special Gestapo commission begins investigation and mass arrests in wake of coup attempt: special wing of Moabit Prison is reserved for suspects; "intensive" interrogation is approved. Baron Ludwig von Leonrod, a member of Heilig Blut Parish, is arrested for participating in July 20 plot.

AUGUST 8: Show trials of those implicated in July 20 coup attempt begin in People's Court.

AUGUST 18: Under torture, Baron von Leonrod reveals that he sought advice from his confessor, Fr. Hermann Joseph Wehrle of Heilig Blut Church. Fr. Wehrle is arrested in Munich.

AUGUST 26: Baron von Leonrod executed at Plötzensee.

SEPTEMBER 14: Fr. Hermann Joseph Wehrle is executed at Plötzensee. [Exaltation of the Cross.]

SEPTEMBER 25: As defeat looms, German civilians are called upon to defend the country. *Volkssturm* (People's Storm) mobilizes all males ages 16 to 60.

OCTOBER 21: Aachen is first German city occupied by U.S. forces.

NOVEMBER 30: With fellow prisoners Eugen Gerstenmaier, Helmuth von Moltke, and Ernst Fugger von Glott, prays a novena for December 8 (Feast of the Immaculate Conception); asks to be granted a sign of God's grace.

DECEMBER 1: Writes two letters, both of which mention that First Fridays, the monthly remembrance of the Sacred Heart of Jesus (as on this date), have always been "special days" in his life.

DECEMBER: *Figures of Advent.*

DECEMBER 3: *Meditation for the First Sunday of Advent.*

DECEMBER 5: Part of Tegel Prison is damaged in air raid; Marianne Hapig meets prison guard, who agrees to help Fr. Delp.

DECEMBER 8: Fr. Delp professes his final vows as a Jesuit in Tegel Prison, Berlin.

DECEMBER 10: *Meditation for the Second Sunday of Advent.*

DECEMBER (mid-month): Has his first meeting with attorney.

DECEMBER 17: *Meditation for the Third Sunday of Advent.*

DECEMBER 24: *Meditation for the Fourth Sunday of Advent and Christmas Vigil.*

DECEMBER 16—JANUARY 21: Belgian counteroffensive; Battle of the Bulge.

1945—JANUARY 9–11: Stands trial before Judge Freisler.

JANUARY 11: Receives guilty verdict and death sentence.

1945—JANUARY: Soviet offensive on the Eastern Front.

JANUARY 11: Jesuit Provincial Augustin Rösch is arrested.

JANUARY 21: German forces are defeated in Belgium; more than 76,000 American soldiers die in the campaign.

JANUARY 23: Moltke, Gross, Sperr, Haubach, and Planck are executed.

JANUARY 30: His last note is smuggled out of Tegel Prison.

JANUARY 31: He is transferred to Plötzensee Prison.

FEBRUARY 2: Fr. Delp is executed by hanging, at Plötzensee Prison, along with Carl F. Goerdeler and Johannes Popitz. [Feast of the Presentation, and First Friday.]

JANUARY 30: Hitler's last radio broadcast.

FEBRUARY 3: Massive Allied air raid over Berlin: People's Court is hit by Allied bomb; Judge Roland Freisler is killed.

FEBRUARY 4–11: Yalta Conference: Roosevelt, Churchill, and Stalin negotiate a postwar plan, including the division of Germany and administration of occupied territories.

MARCH 20: Hitler orders destruction of all German military, transportation, communication, industrial, power, and supply facilities, to prevent Allied forces from using them.

APRIL 8–9: The SS murders Dietrich Bonhoeffer, Klaus Bonhoeffer, Hans von Dohnanyi, and others.

APRIL 9: U.S. forces under General Eisenhower halt 55 miles outside Berlin, to await arrival of Soviet Army.

APRIL 25: Soviet forces surround Berlin.

APRIL 28: In Italy, Mussolini is executed.

APRIL 30: Hitler commits suicide in Berlin bunker.

MAY 2: Soviet forces take Berlin.

MAY 7: War in Europe ends; Germany capitulates.

AUGUST 6, 9: U.S. drops atomic bombs on Hiroshima and Nagasaki.

SEPTEMBER 2: Japan formally surrenders: World War II ends.

APPENDIX II

The Eternal Advent

An Advent play for youths by Alfred Delp, S.J.

Written and performed at Stella Matutina School,
Feldkirch, Austria
December 1933

> *All of you who, in secret longing,*
> *stretch your hands out toward happiness:*
> *One day God's hand will touch you!*
> *One day His hand will come over you,*
> *stroke your hot foreheads,*
> *heal your bleeding wounds,*
> *fill your empty hands.*

— Alfred Delp, S.J.
  The Eternal Advent, Scene 1

CHARACTERS

NARRATOR

Scene 1. The Dead Soldiers

THE SERGEANT
PRIVATE PITT
PRIVATE STONE
PRIVATE CHURCH
PRIVATE SMITH
THE DEAD SOLDIER

Scene 2. The Miners

ENGINEER
FOREMAN
FIRST MINER
SECOND MINER
APPRENTICE

Scene 3. The Worker Priest

PRIEST
DIRECTOR
FOREMAN
WORKERS: HUBER, DRESSEL, HAMMER, ZANDER

The Eternal Advent

An Advent play for youths by Alfred Delp, S.J.

Note to this translation: To close each scene, Alfred Delp selected music that was very familiar and meaningful to his audience. Equivalent, well-known English music has been substituted as follows:

Scene 1: "Taps" replaces "Guten Kamaraden", a song traditionally played at a German soldier's funeral. "O Come, O Come, Emmanuel" replaces "Tauet Himmel", a German Advent hymn.

Scene 2: "This Little Light of Mine" replaces "Das Steigerlied", a cheerful German folk song about following the foreman into the mine: ". . .And he's got his little light in the dark, And he's got his little light in the dark". The hymn "Come, Thou Long-Expected Jesus" replaces the German hymn "O Heiland, reiß die Himmel auf".

Scene 3: No change is necessary here; Delp specified "Das Weihnachts-lied", which in English is "Silent Night".

NARRATOR:

How should we celebrate the holiday
toward which we are hurrying?
May we learn to celebrate it
free of the avalanche of trinkets
with which, all too easily, people bury
the great meaning of this holy day.
May we stand face to face with
the great, holy reality of Christmas.

This holy day toward which we are hurrying
is not just some winter celebration
invented to make children happy.
It is not just a day for giving and receiving
that which gives joy to human eyes and minds.
This day is great and solemn.
Its deeper sense and holy solemnity mean
that God touches us;

that, on this day,
God stepped into our misery
and became our brother.

Let the play begin!

Scene 1. *The Dead Soldiers*

THE SERGEANT
PRIVATE PITT
PRIVATE STONE
PRIVATE CHURCH
PRIVATE SMITH
THE DEAD SOLDIER

> *Advance guard-post on the front line. Soldiers crouch close together around the* SERGEANT. *The* SERGEANT *stands up.*

SERGEANT: Private Pitt, go out about a hundred yards and stand guard. Keep a good lookout. In an emergency, flash a light signal back to us immediately. You'll be relieved in half an hour.

PITT: Yes, sir!

SERGEANT: (*Slaps* PITT's *shoulder.*) See you later, buddy.

PITT: See you later. (*Exits.*)

SERGEANT: At ease. We're secure here. A little talking is okay if we keep it down. Smith, you relieve Pitt in half an hour.

SMITH: Yes, sir!

> *All is quiet. Occasional sound of grenade explosions in the distance. Intermittent shooting. Now and then, a searchlight*

sweeps over the field. As it passes, the soldiers take cover, ducking behind nearby sandbags. Long pause . . .

SMITH: Wonder if we'll make it back alive? It really stinks this time. You can almost feel it, that something's gonna happen.

CHURCH: Lighten up. It'll be over soon enough. How much longer is our watch, Sergeant?

SERGEANT: Another two hours, till midnight.

STONE (*very slowly and dramatically*): Hey, Smith, yesterday, out of one whole watch, nobody made it back! Every single one of 'em dead!

SMITH: They should dig up the whole field here and take it back home for burial—it's soaked full of blood.

CHURCH: You got that right. So many of our guys are getting hit.

A searchlight sweeps over the field, holding for a few moments near the soldiers. They duck, as well as they can. Shots ring out nearby.

STONE: Hey, I got a question—Sergeant, how old are you?

SERGEANT: Why do you want to know?

STONE: Because it seems like there's nothing but young guys out here.

CHURCH: You can look a long time before you find a real old soldier.

SMITH: Almost all the good ones get shot to pieces. And the other ones have landed desk jobs by now. They'll be called up for the commemoration speeches when they dedicate our memorial monument.

STONE: Up there, at that thin line that still calls itself the front—who's lying in the trenches? Mostly young school kids up there. Hey Sergeant, how old were you when the war started?

SERGEANT: Just graduated. Couldn't wait to enlist. I'll never forget that first day. That's when I got an idea of what . . .

PITT (*enters quickly*): Heads up, somebody's sneaking around over there. He's coming toward us.

SERGEANT: Scout?

CHURCH: Probably like the one yesterday who did in the whole watch with a grenade.

SERGEANT: Smith, Pitt, aim your weapons! Stone, Church, grenades ready in case a whole squad is coming. I'll shoot first. Smith, light it up a second!

SMITH *shines a flashlight briefly.* THE SERGEANT *takes aim and fires. A cry is heard, a soft moan, a fall. The moaning gradually becomes weaker. Then all is quiet.*

STONE: Did you see that? Another kid fresh from school. It's the same everywhere.

Pause.

CHURCH: Hey, Smith, any word from home? How's it going?

SMITH: Lousy! Nothing to eat. They're sick. They're hungry, man. Hungry . . .

SERGEANT: Our people—that's what we're fighting for!

STONE: Why does it have to be like this, Sergeant?

SERGEANT: Duty!

CHURCH: Why does duty have to be like this? Why are the best guys dying here at the front, while so many bums are safe at home?

SERGEANT: We're doing our duty here!

SMITH: Why are our families starving at home? Our fathers got shot to pieces, and we're lying here waiting for the same. Why is the world like this, that everybody has such a hard time? Why is it like this?

SERGEANT: It's not our business . . .

In the distance, machine-gun fire picks up. Searchlight passes over soldiers again.

STONE: Look, Sergeant, here's the front line, and our guys are back there, standing and looking out over the trenches. If they see somebody, then they do their duty. Up there is the enemy's front line. And soldiers are standing there too, looking out. If they see somebody, they do their duty. And it goes on like that, all the way up to the sea, and way down to the south. The same in the cold east, up to the mountain peaks. Everybody's doing his duty. They're all defending something that's holy to them. And they're all unhappy, and they're making other people unhappy. Why is duty like this?

CHURCH: Think of the front, Sergeant. How many guys are out here tonight from both sides? They're thinking about the wife and kids, about their mothers, about the families they want to go home to and be happy with. They think about some piece of land they'd like to build on. About the house where they'd like to live a happy life. They're out here dreaming, waiting, and hoping. They're here, holding a cold weapon in the hand, a grenade in the fist, but their hearts want something else. And maybe a hot piece of lead comes along and wipes it all out. And all of them—on both sides— they're all just stretching their hands out toward happiness. They all just want to be happy and content. They all stretch out their hands. But nobody reaches a hand out to meet them. Nobody fills their empty hands with happiness and peace.

Think, you guys—the whole front, both sides, all over the world. (*Speaks slower, softer, trails off.*) They're all secretly stretching out their hands for happiness and nobody . . .

STONE: Did you hear how that guy moaned, a little while ago? How slowly he died? Did he stretch his hand out toward happiness?

CHURCH (*slowly*): They're all secretly stretching their hands out toward happiness . . .

PITT: Hey—enemy battalion extreme right! They're attacking!

SERGEANT: Ready! Fi . . .

In a flash, they are prepared. They are in position, grenades ready, but an enemy grenade hits. Right after the explosion, cries and moans of the wounded are heard.

SMITH *rolls onto his back; doesn't speak anymore. His weapon is clenched in his hand.*

CHURCH (*raises himself halfway up*): They—they're all—
   secretly—stretching their hands out . . . (*Falls on his side.*)

STONE (*cries out*): Ma! —Everybody's—stretching—their . . .
   (*Falls forward.*)

SERGEANT (*lifts himself halfway, with effort*): Who's left?

   Pitt . . . (*No answer.*) . . . dead.

   Smith . . . dead.

   Church . . . dead.

   Stone . . .

STONE: —their hands—out—nobody . . .

SERGEANT: I'm the last one. The report has to get back.
   (*Slowly, wearily, he tries to rise.*) I can't make it. Same as
   yesterday. Nobody makes it back. The best ones have to
   die here—the others have it good at home. They all—
   secretly stretch—their hands out—toward—happiness.
   —Nobody—nobody—nobody . . .

   *He dies. His head falls to his chest; he remains sitting upright,
   leaning against a stone.*

   *The searchlight sweeps over the field again. It holds on the
   group of dead soldiers and then moves to* THE DEAD SOLDIER,
   *who steps out from upstage. He salutes his companions, then
   steps through the midst of them and speaks slowly and formally.*

THE DEAD SOLDIER:

   The column of courageous soldiers extends
   great and wide and far off into the distance.
   They stand faithfully and defiantly at their posts,
   their hands holding weapons, grenades,

reaching for detonators of deadly missiles.
Their hearts are at home with all that is dear to them.
And they are all secretly stretching
their hands out toward happiness.
And nobody takes their hands.

The column of dead soldiers extends
great and wide and far off into the distance.
They lie silent and still beneath the cool earth.
They rot in grenade craters,
their bodies torn by shrapnel.
Their loved ones pine away with worry;
their children are wasting away;
their houses lie in ruins.
As they once did in life, so now from their graves,
they are all secretly stretching
their hands out toward happiness.
And nobody grasps their hands.

Someday a moment will come;
a hand will reach out
from another world,
will reach in from another life,
and will grasp all the hands
that ever stretched themselves
out toward happiness.
It will be the hand of God, and yet
the hand of the most faithful brother.

Dead soldiers, and you who live
because they died here,
all of you who, in secret longing,
stretch your hands out toward happiness:
one day God's hand will touch you!

One day His hand will come over you,
stroke your hot foreheads,
heal your bleeding wounds,
fill your empty hands.
All of you who secretly stretched out your hands
toward happiness:
someday, someone will come
and take your hand!

The melody of "Taps" plays softly, segueing into "O Come, O Come, Emmanuel" as the stage lights dim. The curtain falls.

Scene 2. *The Miners*

ENGINEER
FOREMAN
FIRST MINER
SECOND MINER
APPRENTICE

End of a tunnel. Sound of a drill is heard. An electric light bulb hangs from the low ceiling. Picks and shovels are lying around the perimeter. MINERS *and* FOREMAN *enter, wearing blue overalls. They silently begin working. After a short time, the* ENGINEER *enters. Sound of drilling continues. The* ENGINEER *signals the* FOREMAN.

ENGINEER: Looks like there's not much we can do here. You haven't found anything?

FOREMAN: Only traces, Chief. All the rest is solid rock.

ENGINEER: We're going to shut this tunnel down. See to it that you take as many of these used support beams as you can out of here to use in the new tunnel. The new

one runs parallel to this one and makes a turn opposite
seam Number Eight.

FOREMAN: Right, Chief. Man, I'm glad we're getting out
of here. We've had a few really bad days every year in
this tunnel.

ENGINEER: Let's not even talk about that. Good luck!

*They shake hands. In the same moment, a muffled crash is
heard from far off. The lights dim. The drill slows. The miners
look stunned.*

ENGINEER: Get the testing equipment! Check the air for
gas!

APPRENTICE (*calls from offstage*): Look out! Explosion alert!
Across from Tunnel Eleven!

FOREMAN: That's us!

ENGINEER: Hey! Hello! Over here!

APPRENTICE (*rushing in*): The shaft caved in up there! The
way to the mine elevator is filled up. Tunnel Seven is
totally blocked!

ENGINEER: Come on, get to work! Grab the picks and
shovels! Let's see what we can do!

APPRENTICE: The explosion alert, Chief . . .

*Suddenly the electric light goes out completely. The beams give
way. Rubble pours down on the workers as they fall to the
ground. After the noise, everything is quiet for a moment. The
only light comes from the lanterns, flickering like votive lights.
After a few moments, a metal tool drops to the ground with a
clang.*

FIRST MINER: Are you okay? Are you still there? (*He crawls around and bumps into the* ENGINEER.)

ENGINEER (*speaking slowly*): What is it? Oh, yeah, the explosion! Where is everybody?

FIRST MINER: Maybe they . . .

ENGINEER: No, go look! Right now!

They shine their lanterns, clear away the rubble. The FOREMAN *sits up.*

FIRST MINER: My partner's dead—Smitty. That beam crushed his skull.

FOREMAN: Where's the kid—the apprentice? I used to work with his dad, you know.

ENGINEER (*keeps looking*): Here—he's lying here. Under the beam. (*They move it off him.*) Do you have anything to drink?

FOREMAN (*pulls out a canteen*): Here, take this.

ENGINEER: Just a little for the kid here. (*They give him a drink. He sits up.*)

FIRST MINER: You okay, kid? Don't worry, everything will be all right.

ENGINEER: Come on, let's get back to work! We have to check things out and see what we can do to save ourselves. (*Inspects the perimeter of the tunnel. Finally he speaks, sounding discouraged.*) There isn't much we can do. The bulkheads are solid rock. If the veins of coal were wider, we could try to work our way through to the next tunnel. Or the others could get through to us a lot easier.

MINER (*very agitated*): We have to shovel out the entrance, as long as our strength holds out. The oxygen will run out. If we don't do something, we'll suffocate. (FOREMAN *gets the shovels.*)

ENGINEER (*speaks calmly*): Let me take a look first. (*He works on the debris blocking the entrance. Speaks again, slowly.*) This has to stay as it is. The groundwater is rising out there. The pumps don't seem to be running. If we move this dirt, the water will rush in and flood this area. We have to wait for them to get us out, or . . .

MINER (*upset*): Or . . . or . . . or what?

ENGINEER (*points to the dead man*): How old was he?

FOREMAN: Thirty!

ENGINEER: Any family?

FOREMAN: Wife, two sons. Nice guy. Now they're up there waiting at the entrance for their dad.

MINER *groans loudly.* FOREMAN *takes all the lanterns and places them center stage in a small circle.*

APPRENTICE: Why are you doing that?

FOREMAN: I want to see people one more time, before . . . —with the same longing burning in their eyes, like mine, before . . .

ENGINEER (*takes a flashlight and hangs it from a beam so the whole group is lighted*): That'll keep shining for a half an hour!

MINER (*looks at his watch*): Right now, the movie's starting up there. (*His inner anguish is noticeable, but he speaks slowly.*) I went to see it last Sunday. First came the previews. The last one showed a big wedding parade in Rome. Thousands of people on their way to church. They all looked happy, and joyful music was playing. (*Increasingly emotional, and more slowly.*) Then the feature started. Really funny comedy. Fantastic! A guy, just like one of us, works his way out of the gutter and makes it to the top! It's called *Jack's in Luck!* I wanted to see it again today. (*Pointing to the dead miner.*) Smitty wanted to go with me. *Jack's in Luck!* Here are the tickets! (*Rips them up and throws them away.*) And now, here we are . . .

ENGINEER: Don't give up hope; maybe they'll get us out before it's too late. You know the guys up there are doing everything they can to get us out.

FOREMAN: Maybe! Maybe!

APPRENTICE: My mom's waiting supper for me at home. She always waits for me now, ever since my dad didn't make it out of Pit Level Fifteen.

Pause. All are silent . . .

MINER *stands up, runs back and forth in agitation, then sits down, muttering to himself in distress.*

APPRENTICE: Tonight I was supposed to go to my youth group meeting. Jack, our group leader, was going to tell about one of his trips. He's led so many great trips. I went on one last May, a boat-ride down the river. All the trees were in blossom, the people were laughing, so happy and content. It was really very nice.

Pause. All are silent. ENGINEER *looks at his watch.*

APPRENTICE: The bulletin board had a notice that tonight's meeting would be about traveling around the world.

(*Pause. All are silent.*) Hey, Chief. You know so many things. You must know—why does everybody want to be happy all the time?

MINER (*tortured*): Be quiet!

ENGINEER: That's just the way it is, kid.

APPRENTICE: How long does it last? Does it stop when you get older? Does it stop if, like, we don't get out of here?

FOREMAN: Ralph, it never stops, never! Did you ever see how kids from our neighborhood look when they go down a street lined with big department stores? They stand there and press their little noses flat on the display windows and look with their little eyes at all the pretty things their hearts are yearning for. (*Pause. All are silent.*) That's how it is for all of us. All our lives, we have a heart full of longing and homesickness. Our whole lives, it's like we're standing in front of a display window, looking in.

APPRENTICE: But someday, it has to be that . . .

MINER (*suddenly interrupts, cries out*): We have to get out of here! We have to get out of here! I can't stand it anymore! (*He shakes the side beam.*)

ENGINEER: Stop that!

MINER: I have to get out! I have to! (*Shakes the supporting beam again.*)

Another cave-in follows. Beams, rocks, and dirt fall on the workers. The lanterns go dark, except for one. It's quiet again.

APPRENTICE (*very slowly, word by word*): But someday, it has to be that the window opens. Someday, someone has to fulfill that yearning—that longing that doesn't ever die, even if we don't get out of here.

FOREMAN: Believe me, boy—someday, someone will come and quiet the longing. Boy, do you hear me? (*Pause. Silence.*) Am I the last one? Way down here? I'm saying what everybody feels, deep down inside. Someday there has to be an end to this waiting and hoping. Believe me, I've sensed it all my life. All my life, I've been looking through that window. Not just for things from this world. Them too—I've wanted them too. But that's not all. Our hearts are always full of yearning and homesickness. Believe me, boy. Believe me, everybody. Earthly things don't give your heart peace. Someday, somebody will come and open all the windows and doors, and look at us with holy eyes. He will touch our hearts with healing hands. Someday, someone has to come. I've waited for Him all my life.

The last lantern goes dark. Softly, melody of "This Little Light of Mine" begins, then segues into "Come, Thou Long-Expected Jesus".

Scene 3. *The Worker Priest*

THE PRIEST
THE DIRECTOR
THE FOREMAN
WORKERS: HUBER, DRESSEL, HAMMER, ZANDER

Factory entrance. A siren signals the end of the workday. Sounds of tools being laid aside. A group of workers enters, conversing with each other. Near the entrance to the factory is a scrap heap—scrap metal, etc.

HAMMER: Someone should blow the whole thing up. It's always the same thing, win or lose, good times or bad times! The rich get richer, and the poor get poorer!

FOREMAN: Now, don't be hasty, Hammer. You shouldn't take things so hard. It will all work out for the best.

DRESSEL: Oh, cut it out! Being reasonable has come over you as suddenly as your new promotion. Younger than we are and already a foreman. I guess the bosses knew what they were doing when they picked you . . .

FOREMAN: Shut up! I won't stand for that kind of . . .

HUBER: But you've got to admit it's all wrong. The new machine hasn't been tested enough yet. And so far, every time it's been tried there's been an accident. And tomorrow the whole shift will be working with it.

ZANDER: It's always the same. Look at how it was during the war! The guys at the front had the spirit. They really risked their necks for their country. But back here, management made a business out of patriotism, and when the war was over, they built up new factories on the tombs of the heroes.

HAMMER: I'm going to tell the workers and the committee that it would be better to shut down the factory than to operate that new machine. We don't want to take any chances.

The group becomes increasingly agitated. Sounds of tools being put away and departure of workers continue to be heard.

FOREMAN: Just don't do anything rash. We want to work together on this . . .

ALL: Oh, sure! Anyone can see that! Company puppet! Let's "work together" right now, and beat him up!

They grab pieces of scrap metal from the nearby scrap heap. The DIRECTOR *enters, ready to leave for the day, wearing coat, hat, carrying a briefcase.*

DIRECTOR (*sharply*): Oh, here's a pretty sight! My own people stirring up trouble right here on company property.

FOREMAN: Excuse me, sir. It isn't as bad as it looks. They're a little upset about the new machine, because it hasn't been . . .

DIRECTOR: Not another word! I'm not changing my mind. Tomorrow the new machine goes on line. By the way, Foreman, what are you doing here? Did I raise you up from the blue-collar gutter just for this? I'm telling you, the machine starts tomorrow! Anybody who doesn't like it doesn't have to work here anymore.

The workers are intimidated at first, and then begin to raise their clubs menacingly.

ZANDER: Only one thing to do, fellows. Let's get down to business!

DIRECTOR: Not one more word! Foreman, you call the police! I want the start-up to be secure, no matter what! And nothing is to get in the way of that!

The FOREMAN *stands in front of the workers, who are silent and filled with rage.*

HAMMER: We're calling a shop meeting right now. It's time to make a decision.

DIRECTOR: I'm the one making the decisions. Foreman, did you understand my instructions? Get to it!

During this last exchange, a PRIEST *has come quickly, yet without showing undue haste, from the street to the yard. At first, he stands in the background and observes the situation. After the last word of the* DIRECTOR:

PRIEST (*to the* FOREMAN): Should you really report this to the police? Wait just a moment! (*Turns to the* DIRECTOR.) What luck to run into you here, sir! I was just on my way to see you. I had heard that there was a disagreement between you and your people. Perhaps I can be of service in preventing anything extreme.

DIRECTOR (*first silent, then laconic*): In our position, we can't make allowances . . .

PRIEST: Then at least let me speak with your people, before this gets out of hand.

DIRECTOR: Fine! (*Exits.*)

FOREMAN: I'm warning you, Father, these folks are pretty riled up. Things could easily get out of control.

PRIEST (*to the workers*): Okay, what's going on, folks? What's the problem?

HAMMER: There's no point, Father. You can spare yourself the trouble.

DRESSEL: It's nothing but an act. It's the same everywhere. The ones who have it good stick together against the others, who only get to watch from the sidelines.

FOREMAN: Now be reasonable, you guys.

HAMMER: Aren't you fed up yet? You just heard how he "promoted you out of the blue-collar gutter".

PRIEST: Now just hear me out, folks. Together we need to think of some way . . .

HAMMER: Easy for you to talk. You've got a warm room to go to. You've got enough to eat, and no hungry mouths to feed. But we're going to be fired three weeks before Christmas, because we refuse to shut up and put up with unsafe conditions.

HUBER: You always talk about dialogue, Father. But there comes a time for action. A lot of things have to change!

PRIEST (*calmly and firmly*): Yes, many things need to change. At the top and here below. We have to start with ourselves. Here inside is where it has to start (*points to his heart*).

DRESSEL: We aren't satisfied with that, Father. We want to see real changes.

ZANDER: You've got it too good, Father. Otherwise, you wouldn't talk like that. You don't know what it's like for us.

PRIEST: We have to come to terms, folks. Otherwise, the police will be called, and things will only get worse.

HAMMER (*totally out of control*): Now *you* want to call in the police, too! He's on their side! Did you all hear that? Let him be the first one . . .

The workers raise their clubs. Someone shouts: "He's one of them!" As they move to attack the PRIEST, *the lights briefly go out. As the lights come on, the* PRIEST *collapses. The* FOREMAN

*catches him and lays him on the ground near an empty packing
case.*

FOREMAN (*while tending the priest*): You guys! . . . What have
you done?

The workers' agitation changes to remorseful silence.

PRIEST: You said I had it too good. That's all over now. So
now, at least believe what I have to tell you . . .

DRESSEL: Father, we didn't mean for this to happen. (*He
drops his stick.*)

PRIEST: Don't. It's all right. People shouldn't have it too
good. That way, they keep watching for the other, for
what's better. They always have to keep stretching their
hands out toward that other happiness. They always need
to have a hungry heart. That is what needs to change
first of all—inside each one of us. (*Pause.*)

FOREMAN: But a lot of things in the world have to change
too! There's so much injustice, the way things are.

PRIEST: Yes, there's a lot of injustice. Many things in the
world have to change too, but first on the inside.
Otherwise, it won't be right on the outside. It only
turned bad outside in the world, because things weren't
right inside of us.

HAMMER (*still angry, but no longer so out of control*): But it's
wrong to put us out of work, right before Christmas.
Think of our children. How will they celebrate
Christmas?

PRIEST: How should your children celebrate Christmas?
How should you celebrate Christmas? It isn't right.

What they are doing to you isn't right, but the other isn't right, either—what you are doing.

HUBER: What other?

PRIEST: How it is inside of you. Christmas is coming soon. And what does Christmas mean to you?

ZANDER: It's the children's celebration. They are already looking forward to it. And we look forward to it, too, to see them so happy. That's why it's so hard to accept what's going on.

PRIEST: The children's celebration. Oh, yes, and we give chocolate Santas and toy soldiers and Christmas cookies. That's how it is with the little ones, the poor. For the rich it goes farther: fur coats, new cars, et cetera. And that's Christmas, right? So a lot really needs to change.

DRESSEL: Yeah, at least everyone should have enough to eat.

PRIEST: Yes, everyone should have enough to eat. But, tell me, is that Christmas? Is that Christmas? (*Pause. All are silent.*) When the Christmas bells are ringing . . . (*softly, church bells begin to ring*) . . . is the only thing ringing inside you just the longing for things out there? (*Pause. All are silent.*) Yes, many things have to change. It won't be good for me anymore. I still want to tell you what you need to do, quickly, before it's finished. There's a book in my pocket. Give it to me. (*They give him his Breviary from his pocket.*) Believe me, I'm telling you what I know, and what I believe, and what will make you happy. You see, Christmas is not about cute trinkets and pretty packages. Christmas is first of all here, inside. Listen. This is Christmas (*reads from his Breviary*):

"The people sitting in misery, and living in deep, bitter distress, to this people will come a great light."

"Behold, the Lord will come, and on that day a great peace will come over the earth."

"The Messiah is born to you today, the Savior and Redeemer."

Church bells ring louder; the PRIEST *speaks more and more slowly, gently.*

My dear friends, that is Christmas—that a hand from above reaches into our lives and touches our hearts. That is Christmas, not the other things. My friends, believe it, we have to suffer a lot and hang on. Only then is it Christmas.

Christmas is not a sweet fairytale for little children—for happy nurseries . . . Christmas is serious—so serious—that men gladly—die for it. —Tell everyone—many things have to change—first—here—inside . . .

Christmas means that God—touches us,—that He—grasps our hands—and lays them—on—His—heart. —That God comes—to us—and sets us free. —Tell everyone—the other isn't Christmas,—only this—is—Christmas,—that—God—is—with—us.

The PRIEST *sinks down. The Christmas bells ring out loud and clear, as the melody of "Silent Night" begins to play.*

APPENDIX III

Advent 1935

This threefold meaning of Advent basically expresses the entire intrinsic meaning of Christianity:
— the relation and vocation of all people to God, as well as guidance and providential direction through God;
— the redeeming fulfillment in Christ; and
— the continuation and application of the redemption through the Church of Christ.

— Alfred Delp, S.J.
   "Advent 1935"

The following sermon sketch is the first of a series written for the weekly homiletic publication *Chrysologus*. The editor of *Chrysologus* was Fr. Jakob Nötges, S.J. (1880–1963). He was also professor of homiletics at Valkenburg and often gave students an opportunity to work on the publication. He entrusted the issues for the year 1936 to Alfred Delp. The focus of the 1936 series was an examination of the pagan and Aryan-based "German Faith Movement", which had been growing in popularity since 1932. Delp planned the series and wrote eleven of the thirty-eight published sermons.

ADVENT 1935

The first sermon of this series about reflection and decision comes at the beginning of Advent. For the believer, the season of Advent is always a time of reflection and interior turning toward God, who is the homeland of our hearts. At the beginning of Advent, we want to provide our people with a clear view of the actual religious and Church situation.

1. Christian Advent

The believing Christian celebrates an Advent with multiple meanings. Each of these meanings ultimately leads to generally applicable religious principles and problems. Therefore Advent is precisely the liturgical season in which the interior religious tension of our time is most conspicuously revealed.

a. The season of Advent is, first of all, the time of man's original religious instinct. Never will we experience our primeval homesick yearning for God more actively and alertly than in this season of Rogation Masses and Advent wreaths. Advent is the time of the God-seeker. The original longing within every human heart is a great impulse toward the hidden and distant God, a longing to wander in that far-off, forgotten homeland of the soul. That longing is what the Church expresses, both in her inner attitude and in the liturgy of this season.

b. Beyond this general human meaning, Advent has a great historical meaning to the believer, the grateful remembrance of the millennia of God's gracious care that has led man to the fulfillment of this longing for Him. Thus the season of Advent clearly reveals the basic meaning of all human events and historical developments: man's way to God, guidance by God, fulfillment in Christ.

c. In conclusion: The believing Christian celebrates Advent in the context of liturgy. By taking part in the inner life of the Church, he expresses within himself, within his life, the original religious and historical meaning of Advent. He lets himself be caught up in that "fullness of time", which is both actually present and always returning, within the Church of Christ.

This threefold meaning of Advent basically expresses the entire intrinsic meaning of Christianity: the relation and vocation of all people to God, as well as guidance and providential direction through God; the redeeming fulfillment in Christ; and the continuation and application of the redemption through the Church of Christ.

2. Modern Advent 1935

Our present time is, in its fundamental principles, aloof from every human Advent attitude.

a. The original religious meaning of Advent is rejected. People believe they no longer need a divine homeland to which to immigrate. God is within them; they are ultimately God themselves; and there is no God above them.

> The objective power to which we bow, the religious leader to whom we offer obedience, is the religious primeval will of the German people. . . . We have no other creed than the duty to this religious primeval will. . . . To this primeval will, we are unconditionally committed (Hauer, *Was will die deutsche Glaubensbewegung?* p. 19).

> This religious primeval will, which is absolutely valid and binding, is nothing other than the singularity of the German

people, according to their race and blood (ibid.; also Hauer,
Deutsche Gottschau, pp. 45ff.).

For German faith, human events are the same as acts of God.
Uniting as a people is the same as the embodiment of the will
of God (*Deutsche Gottschau*, p. 65).[1]

These citations do not intend to say that a God from beyond
created this world. Here, God is the final content of all being,
and there is no ultimate difference between God and the
"created world". God is the "eternal self" that lives within all
things. Moreover, these things neither exist above and beyond this self, nor is the self above and beyond the things.
"The Aryan view of the world does not differentiate between
this world and the next" (Reventlow, *Wo ist Gott?* p. 310).
Both man and the German people must accept themselves as
the ultimate reality, with all their questionable qualities and
fragility. For the German who subscribes to this faith, no
Advent bells are ringing, and no homeland-garden of God is
calling him to set out on a journey.

   b. The historical meaning of the Christian Advent is rejected. That ancient history of mankind has nothing to do
with the German people. That idea of waiting for Christ does
not touch us. The coming of Christ, the "fullness of time", is
perhaps, in itself, a religious event for other people—but not
for us, under any circumstances. The ancient history of religion, faith in revelation, salvation of the world: all these are
conclusions drawn from a world essentially foreign to us;

[1] The authors and works to which Fr. Delp refers in the text are (1) JAKOB
WILHELM HAUER (1881–1926), leader of the German Faith Movement,
professor in Marburg and Tübingen (publications: *Was will die deutsche Glau-
bensbewegung?* [Stuttgart: Verlag Hirschfeld, 1934], and *Deutsche Gottschau*
[Stuttgart: Verlag Gutbrod, 1934]); and (2) ERNST GRAF ZU REVENTLOW
(1869–1943), politician (publication: *Wo ist Gott?* [Berlin: Verlag Reichswart,
1934]).

products of Syrian-Semitic faith and the oriental races (*Gottschau*, pp. 4ff.). Only the Middle-Easterner is a "person of the redemption"—a German does not have such needs.

c. The liturgical meaning of Christian Advent is rejected. It makes no sense to desire to come closer to God through participation in the inner life of the Church. The entire life of the Church is Etruscan-Syrian fiction. Even there where the Church is granted a religious value in itself and for other peoples and races, this value for the German people is denied.

> There is for us no higher revelation of eternal reality than within the German sphere and from the German soul. The religious primeval will of the German people is to us the will of eternal reality that comes to us in the form of faith, in the measure appropriate to our being. Our highest destiny is to live within and embody this form, which for the sake of the will of our people, we have to fulfill (Hauer, *Was will die deutsche Glaubensbewegung?* p. 22).

The German faith knows no articulated Creed, no dogma, no form, it cannot be "enclosed within any church" (ibid., p. 18).

> The idea of the Church has nothing to do with the German people, nor the Aryan people, insofar as they have kept themselves pure. It stands in opposition to their traditions, as well as to their identity (Reventlow, *Wo ist Gott?* p. 43).

> Worship services, sacraments, rituals—to the German all of these are foreign goods forced upon us by a foreign race (Reventlow, *Wo ist Gott?* pp. 40ff.).

Even where they accept a real connection between the historical Christ and His Church, where the Church is seen not merely as the result of a priestly will for power, the Church institutions and establishments are viewed as inappropriate for the German people: Christ is no more capable than we are of overstepping the bounds of sphere and race. It makes no sense for the German to let himself be seized by some inner life of the Church of Christ, to let himself be led by the Church to the source of all eternal life. The Advent bells from our church towers are seductive voices. The "Rorate Cæli" hymn is a confession of individual weakness and an admission of individual helplessness, something that never comes into question for the "Aryan".

3. Decision

The Advent church bells ringing in the midst of this situation are, more than ever, an invitation as well as a call to consciousness and inner recollection. Above and beyond that, they are a call for individual decision. Each one of us is confronted with the new religious ideas in one form or another. It is not enough to be faithful within the privacy of your own heart or home. This is the moment for public, serious, and faithful profession of our faith.

This series of sermons we are beginning is intended to educate, strengthen, and prepare people for this decision. One by one, the basic truths of Christianity and a Christian life will be discussed. One by one, the terminology of the new attempt at religion will be examined. The meaning of the whole, however, is that we want to make a genuine religious decision, and we want to maintain our religious loyalty courageously.

BIBLIOGRAPHY

Bleistein, Roman, S.J. *Alfred Delp: Geschichte eines Zeugen.* Frankfurt am Main: Verlag Josef Knecht, 1989.

———. *Begegnung mit Alfred Delp.* Frankfurt am Main: Verlag Josef Knecht, 1994.

———. *Alfred Delp—Widerstand gegen den Nationalsozialismus.* Munich: Institut für Kommunikation und Medien, 1994.

Delp, Alfred. *Alfred Delp: Kämpfer, Beter, Zeuge.* 3rd ed. Edited by Marianne Hapig. Berlin: Morus-Verlag, 1978.

———. *Der mächtige Gott.* Edited by Paul Bolkovac. Frankfurt am Main: Verlag Josef Knecht, 1949.

———. *Der Mensch im Advent.* Edited by Roman Bleistein, S.J. Frankfurt am Main: Verlag Josef Knecht, 1984.

———. *Gesammelte Schriften.* 5 vols. Edited by Roman Bleistein, S.J. Frankfurt am Main: Verlag Josef Knecht, 1982–1984, 1988.

———. *Im Angesicht des Todes.* Edited by Paul Bolkovac, S.J. 9th ed. Frankfurt am Main: Verlag Josef Knecht, 1965.

———. *Zur Erde entschlossen.* Edited by Paul Bolkovac, S.J. Frankfurt am Main: Verlag Josef Knecht, 1949.

Hammerich, Peter, ed. *Reden und Ansprachen zum Gedenken an Pater Alfred Delp S.J.* 4 vols. Lampertheim: Hammerich, 1975, 1985, 1994, 2000.

Kempner, Benedicta Maria, *Priester vor Hitlers Tribunalen.* Munich: Rütten und Loening Verlag, 1966.

Leber, Annedore. *Das Gewissen steht auf: Lebensbilder aus dem deutschen Widerstand von 1933-1945.* 10th ed. Berlin: Mosaik Verlag, 1954.

Leber, Annedore, and Freya von Molte. *Für und Wider: Entscheidungen in Deutschland 1918–1945*. Berlin: Mosaik Verlag, 1961.

Moll, Helmuth, ed. *Zeugen für Christus: Das deutsche Martyrologium des 20. Jahrhunderts*. 2 vols. Paderborn: Verlag Ferdinand Schöningh, 1999.

Neufeld, Karl H., S.J. *Die Brüder Rahner: eine Biographie*. Freiburg im Breisgau: Verlag Herder, 1994.

Zimmerman, Erich, and Hans-Adolf Jacobsen, eds. *20. Juli 1944*. 3rd ed. Bonn: Berto-Verlag, 1960.

INDEX

Absolute, 39, 62–63, 94, 126, 132.
See also Ultimate
abundance, 23, 30, 95, 101, 104
Advent, meaning of, 39, 50, 62,
66, 72
adoration, 75, 81, 165
Aesop, 143n5
Alexander the Great, 94
angels
of Advent, 26–27
of annunciation, 24, 25–27
approaching, 45
of jubilation, 26, 30
as messengers, 26–27, 29
singing, 160, 164
answers, 39, 79, 93, 145, 151. See
also questions
anxiety, 40, 41, 66, 131, 150. See
also fear
arrogance
autarkical, 111
cannot affect ultimate reality, 40
and caprice, 51
cries of self-importance and, 30
isolation and, 108
modern, 75
night of, 142
pedestals of, 108
remove from our lives, 63
sin of, 131
Augustine, Saint, 107
Augustus Caesar, 94

autarchy, 72, 108
authenticity, 63–66, 92, 114, 126,
132
awakening
being shaken and, 23, 41, 67
grace and, 72
interior agitation and, 80
the Lord calls to, 46
prerequisites for, 70
from sleep, 42
of spirits, minds, and hearts, 100
terror and, 52

barque of the Lord God, 169. See
also ship of life
battlefields, 30
blessing
of Advent, 24, 29
of God, 28, 73, 112, 170
the Lord's, 100
message of, 25–27
seeds of, 26–27
bomb, 26
boundaries, 42, 51, 94, 98, 109.
See also limitations; limits
breath
deep, 107–8, 161
first, 116
of God, 166
of life, 114
of relief (respirare), 160–61, 169
of the soul, 74

225